THE COMPLETE LURCHER

The author's noted show lurcher, a useful coursing dog and a good looker

THE COMPLETE LURCHER
A MANUAL

D. Brian Plummer

Illustrated by Martin Knowelden

The Boydell Press

© D. B. Plummer 1979
First published 1979 by The Boydell Press Ltd
PO Box 9, Woodbridge, Suffolk IP12 3DF

British Library Cataloguing in Publication Data

Plummer, David Brian
  The complete lurcher.
  1. Lurcher
  I. Title
  636.7'53   SF429.L87
  ISBN 0-85115-118-3

Photoset and printed in Great Britain by
Lowe & Brydone Printers Limited, Thetford, Norfolk

CONTENTS

LIST OF ILLUSTRATIONS

Introduction

If it is your wish merely to own a dog of the running-dog variety to walk up a hare, with dog on slip, releasing the dog as the hare is given or denied law (depending on your idea of sportsmanship), allowing it to course the hare and then maybe kill it, I suggest you put this book back on the bookshop shelf (no bookshop owner will be upset by your browsing) and invest your money and time elsewhere. A suitable investment might be a coursing greyhound in preference to a lurcher, and a five-year-old child to train it – correction, perhaps an eight-year-old child as a coursing greyhound is a powerful beast – but a five-year-old child really could master the skill in training such an animal. Do not be ashamed of your lack of ambition in wanting only to own such a dog, for 90 per cent of all lurchermen are the same, requiring nothing more of their dog than the trick I have outlined above. Coursing greyhounds or salukis would suit them equally well. Replace the book on the shelf, in that case, it is not for you.

Should you, however, be that relic of the past, that almost extinct creature, the hunter, and should you require your lurcher, as Dan Russell once said to me, to have the body of a greyhound and the head of a Solomon, to be capable of retrieving any quarry of suitable size, working long nets and gate nets, coursing and lamping, perhaps this may be the book you are looking for. You have one more chance to conserve your money and time and decide not to buy or borrow this work. The training programme is long and hard. The book has been written in tears, not ink. It is a list of my own errors, my own mistakes, with just a sprinkling of my own successes. It has been written by a man out of place in time, old-fashioned enough to expect a lot from a greyhound-blooded dog and is meant for similar out-of-place people. It has also been written in the hope that it may do something to prevent the lurcher degenerating into a poor-grade coursing greyhound – rougher of coat perhaps, but an animal no more trainable than the greyhound. You still have time to replace the book and disagree with my viewpoint, state that I ask too much from a coursing dog; still time not to spend the price of such a book. Decided to go on, have you? Well, yours the money and time, mine the advice.

My work is, I admit, an odd mixture of folk legend which has been placed under the scrutiny of scientific tests. Some of the tests have been conducted by me, others by Brian Broom in the United States. Do not let the word 'science' put you off, reader: hunting itself is a science. Decided to buy or borrow and read on, have you? Then as Shakespeare says, 'Damned be him that first cries, "Hold, enough"' – and this, reader, will be my first and last quote from Shakespeare, a writer with whom, my friends tell me, I am besotted.

1 *The Legendary Norfolk Lurcher*

Now here was a beast, if the legends and lore of the eighteenth century are true, or even half-true – here was a beast that must have been the last word in sporting dogs. Brave, bold, a scent hunter, trainable and fast, the doyen of them all – that is, if legend and lore are true. It might, however, be best to investigate a little of the dog's history and the times that allowed its creation before going into details of its hunting prowess and sagacity, for circumstances and needs create a dog, and man seldom sets out to produce a breed. Breeds occur, brought about by necessity.

Norfolk – a land rich in hares equal to Lincolnshire as a county of coursing potential; but the fat pastures that nurtured these hares also produced plump cattle, sheep, pigs and geese, as well as the turkeys newly imported from America, half-wild and even more difficult to control than the present-day birds. Norfolk – a county of fat beasts that found a ready market in the growing city of London; a market in the famous (or infamous) Smoothfield (later to be altered to Smithfield). London, was, however, a hundred miles away along roads roughly cobbled, ill-kept, and along lanes rarely hedged as they were in the Midlands. Train transport had yet to come, so the beasts were driven from Norfolk to London along the self-same roads that Will Kemp the Clown danced from London to Norwich, roads that in winter had ruts that once drowned a coach and horses.

Farmers rarely themselves drove their produce south as this was the task given to that most controversial of men: the drover. He could be patient when he wished, for the mixed flocks of cattle, sheep and pigs moved slowly, and slowly meant a few miles a day. 'Seven miles a day was the sheep herder's way', said the Australian poet, Banjo Paterson. Push them faster, not allowing them to graze the verges along the route, and they would arrive in Smithfield too thin to sell. Geese, their feet tarred and sanded, and turkeys wearing little boots of leather to resist the hardship of the roads, moved even more slowly. It required a patient drover to accompany such a flock. Not all were patient, however. In the nineteenth century, one, driven to fury by his

11

sheep which were as frisky as autumn adolescent lambs usually are, was maddened by the fact that they leapt the hedges alongside the road. So in the stockyard of one of the numerous inns, called, ironically, the Drover's Rest, he set to and cut the feet off his sheep, driving them the rest of the way to market on the stumps of their legs. The Society for the Prevention of Cruelty to Animals was powerless. Animals had no rights, neither did the society. So, in desperation, they prosecuted the drover for leaving litter on the highway – the feet of the sheep.

To drive livestock a hundred or so miles is no job for one man alone. Any drover who intended to stay in business needed dogs. Herding dogs of a kind were absolutely essential, and they needed to be a strange type of herding dog at that. They had to be larger than the border collie, for they had not only to herd sheep, but also bullocks and even the aged crotchety bulls that were driven into London some six weeks before Christmas for the bull baiting, when a bull was torn to pieces by bulldogs and the flesh that survived this outrageous spectacle was given to the poor. Such were the wards of the dogs, but in addition to these, they must also cope with turkeys and geese in the drives, and these could be driven to feathery hysteria by the actions of an aggressive dog. Hence the Smithfield collie, as these dogs were known, had the same odd mixture of qualities as did their owners.

From the descriptions of the times, these dogs were fairly large, lean, beasts, rough and long of coat, for they slept on the leeward side of the hedge if possible, lying among the cattle if there was no shelter. Tough animals were prized, and those who were constitutionally weak went to the wall. Thus the drover drove his mixed herds to London – the London beloved by Dickens and Mayhew: a cruel, heartless city, though no better nor worse than the rest of the country at that time. The abattoirs into which the sheep were driven were twenty feet below the level of the roads, and for good purpose. Kellow Chesney, in his magnificent book *The Victorian Underworld* (1970), says that the sheep were driven into these pits so that their legs would be broken by the fall, so rendering them easy for the killing. There were no laws to prevent cruelty to animals or children in those days.

With the drovers, their families and the flocks travelled a dog of a different ilk, however. True, their sires and dams were the Smithfield collies, but these other dogs had a liberal addition of greyhound blood in their veins. Besides their herding duties, they were also required to produce meat for the pot. Some had enough greyhound blood to be able to bring down hares. Others were rabbit dogs. All, however, were hunters, for not only did the greyhound blood produce speed and hunting instinct, but their collie ancestors contributed equally to such a mixture. The collie drives its prey towards its master, not to please its owner, but because of a remote instinct that man has harnessed. To the collie, the human owner is a surrogate pack leader, and the collie would be only too delighted if the owner slew the sheep, encouraging his dog to partake in the orgy of blood and destruction. Exaggerated, is that what you think, reader? Then a test is what I ask you to undertake. Watch any sheepdog trial; see how the shepherds find it easy to instruct the dogs to drive sheep towards them, and how difficult it is to get them to drive the same sheep away. Herding is merely hunting instinct gone awry. Border collies and their kin, bored with life and not kept at work, take to sheep worrying far more skilfully and far more destructively, than any other breed of dog.

Thus the wedding of the Smithfield collie and the greyhound gave rise to the more than half-legendary Norfolk lurcher, fast through its greyhound ancestors, cunning through its collie blood. It was the ideal dog of the drover as he passed through estates rich in game, the perfect dog for the poacher during a time when poaching penalties were outlandish: flogging, and even deportation to Botany Bay. It was the provender provider for the artisan hunter bringing up a family truly on the breadline whose only meat was rabbit or hare. It was the scourge of the gamekeeper, who, like William Graham, hated the approach of the drovers' bands with their lurchers; bands who caused havoc in the inns, for a drover's thirst for beer was as legendary as his fighting prowess. It is said that Daniel Mendoza, the fighting Jew, champion of all England, found many a drover a worthy adversary. Graham, however, detested drovers and their dogs, who left behind broken hedges, damage to property and a countryside denuded of game. Graham, the gentlest of men, quite openly set man-traps on his estate during the approach of the droving bands.

Long nets and gate nets were favourite methods of poaching by these bands, for the dogs naturally shepherded prey towards their masters. Their collie blood gave them that instinct, and the massacre of game created by a skilful long netter has to be seen to be believed. Legend or not, these dogs certainly had the breeding to go with the sundry tasks required of them.

Had the ability . . . I have to use the past tense! Times were changing. Not only was the law changing to prevent savage brutality to animals, but the fast-growing towns of the Industrial Revolution were reluctant to tolerate drovers and their wards coming through their streets, leaving mounds of faeces on the road and trouble wherever they went. The trade's death knell was really sounded with the arrival of the railways. Not only was it cheaper to transport live-

13

stock by rail, but the beasts arrived at market in better condition than when they were driven along the roads. The drover became a thing of the past as time went by. Some found employment in the farms along the routes, for their skills with animal husbandry were well regarded. The rest? Well, they were a shiftless lot, nomadic by nature, untrustworthy in the main. They merely joined and swelled the bands of tinkers which filled England's countryside, then as now.

It is interesting to note that gipsies are usually credited with an almost superhuman gift regarding lurcher training – unjustifiably, as it happens. It would be curious to know, and well worth investigating, whether or not it was the English tinker – descended, as he was, from generations of livestock husbandmen – who was the real expert with these dogs. Gipsies and tinkers are both itinerant, and both so alike in dress and transport that even George Borrow, the author of *Lavengro* and *The Romany Rye*, found it difficult to distinguish between them. It is probable that the tinker with his droving ancestors was the real dog trainer.

Thus the drover went the way of the dinosaur: a thing of the past, a relic of a bygone age, interesting, but no longer of use. And even as the drover became displaced, so did his rough, tough, Smithfield collie, for as the drover was replaced by the railways, so was the Smithfield collie replaced by the smaller, less aggressive, herding dogs that eventually gave rise to the Border collie. Perhaps some isolated farmstead in Norfolk still has a specimen or two of this survivor of a bygone age, but it is doubtful, and with the passing of the collie, so the doyens of hunting dogs, the Norfolk lurchers, also died out. Absorbed into sundry other crosses would be a more accurate way of putting it, but they were extinct as surely as if they had died out. From time to time specimens appear at shows, rough in coat, heavy in build, proudly proclaimed as 'genuine Norfolk lurchers', always bred from Smithfield collie/greyhound crosses, but the Smithfield collie went the way of the drover and the dodo. So, it can be assumed, did the Norfolk lurcher.

Man is a curious creature. If the stories of these fabulous hunting dogs were true, and some certainly were, why did he allow them to become extinct? Perhaps the ownership of such a dog was the insignia of the rural ne'er-do-well, the hallmark of the poacher, the night-time skulker. It could be that this pushed the strain of dog over the precipice of extinction, but the bull terrier, the Bill Sykes dog, the dog of the urban ruffians still survives.

Again, I repeat, man is a baffling creature. He allows Przewalski's horse to fall damn nigh into extinction, then strives madly to revive the breed. The Irish wolfhound, useless since wolf and elk became extinct in Britain, had to be reborn from various crosses with allied dogs. So, with the extinction of the Norfolk lurcher, legendary and enigmatic as the chimera itself, man sought to breed other lurchers. He had all the ingredients. There were better greyhounds, faster, gamer, than those the drovers must have used, while collies and sundry other breeds without number were available. Thus he strove to produce a beast to equal, or perhaps better, the Norfolk lurcher. One vital ingredient was missing, however, a catalyst as vital as the philosopher's stone in the making of gold: the type of man with the skill and patience to train these dogs as they should be trained, who would use them as true lurchers, not as poor-grade coursing greyhounds. Their breed had also just about passed into extinction. Few lurchers are exploited to their full today, and fewer still are the men who know how to train these sagacious dogs as they should be. It ought to be the aim of all lurcher breeders and trainers to emulate the skills of those lurchermen of old.

2 *The Modern Lurcher*

To the uninitiated, it must seem a bit of a wonder why man would take a greyhound, a beast of legendary speed, the fastest of all dogs (no matter what unscientific record books say to the contrary), and cross it (ameliorate is a nicer word, though cross will suffice) with another breed to lose some of that staggering speed. Consider the greyhound. Its very shape indicates its speed. It is one of the few dogs that can outrun hare, deer or even antelope. Courage, it has a-plenty, and a greyhound with its dander raised or excited with the chase is damn nigh fearless. So much for its points of excellence. What of its failings and shortcomings? *Stamina* – it has very little. An 800-yard course will render most coursing greyhounds exhausted and out of action for some time. *Scenting ability* – limited, though I have owned greyhounds that would hunt by nose and hunt quite well. Most, however, are strictly sight hounds. *Brain power* – well, now we come to a rather unpleasant truth.

Dogs can be divided into two classes: brachycephalic, meaning broad-headed, and dolicocephalic, meaning narrow-headed. Doli-cocephalic dogs are, without exception, the morons of the dog world. Please disregard any breed books which say that Afghans, grey-hounds and salukis are too intelligent to submit to man's ways or obey him implicitly. Trainability is synonymous with brain power in a dog, and no matter what nonsense such books may say, a dog that cannot be trained, or is untrainable, must be regarded as unintelli-gent. Thus greyhounds, Afghan hounds, salukis and even our native Scottish deerhound, elegant as it is, are all on the very bottom rung of the canine intelligentsia. But having extolled the virtues and enumer-ated the vices of the greyhound and his kin blood, let us examine what the sportsman wants in a lurcher.

Firstly, the dog must be fast – and greyhound blood will usually provide this quality. Secondly, the dog must have stamina for a hard day's coursing. This is a point where most sight-hunting dogs fall short, the saluki being the exception since few dogs are reported to equal them in stamina. Next, it must have courage to continue, even after the odds are very much against it – and greyhounds certainly try hard enough, even if they lack stamina. Lastly, and by no means least, the lurcher must be intelligent: intelligent enough to anticipate the hare's movements, to hunt up game with one eye ever open for the explosion of grass that tells it the prey is running; have brains enough to work a long net, or a gate net if he is very bright, and to work with ferrets (work *with*, I emphasize, not merely stand by the holes like a Diana-the-huntress ornament, elegant, but totally inefficient).

Greyhounds themselves would find such a task beyond them. All sight hounds, without exception, respond to commands with infuriating slowness, a couldn't-care-less attitude that would madden a gun-dog trainer. Most are reluctant to retrieve, and any visit to a coursing meet will find most of the greyhounds there standing over their kill. While it is possible to stunt-train a greyhound to a high standard, and one police force dog trainer has succeeded in achieving excellent results with a track-bred dog, the greyhound still responds with slowness to even simple commands – an infuriating slowness to the hunter, a dangerous slowness to the poacher, and lurchers are the insignia of poachers as much today as they were in the days of the Norfolk drovers. Furthermore, it takes a very long time to train a greyhound in even rudimentary tasks: tasks that a collie would learn in a matter of an afternoon take a sight hound a week to learn properly. Hence it is necessary to ameliorate the greyhound and produce the lurcher. Necessary to cross him with other breeds to give him stamina, the will to go on, and the quality that I personally rate highly – that of nose. Above all, however, and this is a quality of which many lurcher breeders are losing sight, the cross must give the lurcher brains, brains not only to unravel the windings of the hare, but to respond to commands quickly, instantly, to be easily trained, to be, in fact, the all-round hunting dog, the hunter for the kitchen, the provider of the household. Yes, I'll say it again, 'the all-round hunting dog'.

So we have defined exactly what the hunter seeks in his lurcher: brains, stamina and determination, coupled with the speed of the greyhound. Now, however, for a good long look at the greyhound – the starting-point for most lurchers.

3 *The Greyhound*

With justification, this may be regarded as the oldest breed known to man. Carvings of greyhounds, or greyhound-blooded dogs, adorn the tombs of the Pharaohs. Edwardes Clarke describes it as 'as old as time itself' – poetic phrase, and not far wrong. Solomon knew all about its fleetness and praised it. It seems likely that Abraham was well acquainted with these beasts of the chase well before the Lord promised to make him a father of nations, and I suppose it could even be argued by fundamentalists that the two dogs taken by Noah aboard his floating zoo must have been greyhounds. Enough of this speculation, however. He is simply the oldest breed, and as the reader will have gathered, a native of the Middle East.

How he arrived in Britain is an open question. Some say the Phoenicians, when they came trading for tin, offered such dogs as barter to the natives in Britain. Feasible, but somewhat unlikely. More probably the greyhound came in with the Celtic invasions, brought in by those groups who eventually became the ancestors of the Welsh, Irish and Scots. Huge dogs they were, if the tales were true, far bigger than our present-day hounds and heavy-coated as often as not. Nearly every Celtic story tells of them. Rosemary Sutcliffe's books describe them beautifully, and the half-legendary hound of Arthur, Cavall, could have been a large type of greyhound.

It is likely that during the migrations the pure-blooded, smooth-coated dogs, acquired perhaps by trade or warfare from Asia Minor, came to be altered by the addition of other breeds, and that the dogs of the Celts were quite mongrelized when compared with their elegant desert ancestors. One thing is certain. No matter which breeds mingle with greyhound blood, the greyhound type remains dominant, so the Celtic dogs, hairy and huge, were still of greyhound type, no matter how they had changed from their ancestors. Monstrous breeds, these Celtic greyhounds were, capable of killing elk and deer, or fighting alongside their masters as war dogs. Valiant beasts they were as well. If Gelert, the hound of Llewellyn, was true, and not a pseudo-legend to attract tourists to the town of Beddgelert

18

in North Wales, he, too, would have been a greyhound of this type, capable of killing a wolf in single combat.

The Saxons, too, knew of this dog, either through their conquest of the Celts or because they also had dogs of greyhound type. AElfric, the hunting ealdorman of Mercia, hunted both deer and hare with his dogs, and some say was responsible for making the wolf a rarity in Mercia. AElfric of Mercia was an indifferent ruler, perhaps, but a first-rate coursing man whose dogs were as noted for their skill at hare hunting as they were at pulling down wolf and wild boar which then still lived in the acorn forests of Saxon England.

Greyhounds and greyhound types were not the property of nobility alone, however, nor even the exclusive property of the rich. They were also the hunting dogs of the poor. The serf and freeman owned them to provide meat for the table as much as for sport. Class distinction was fairly loose in Anglo-Saxon England, where the very word knight was derived from the Saxon *cnitas*, any man rich enough to own a horse – albeit a scraggy pony.

Times were to change, however. Canute, the first Viking king of England, was decidedly a conservationist – at least where the poor of the land were involved. Concerned by the fact that the peasantry was denuding the country of deer, he passed the first of the notorious Forest Laws, and in 1016 decreed that 'no mean man should own a greyhound'. This, as the first of the Forest Laws, was also the most lenient. Between 1016 and the time of Edward III, some four centuries later, the Forest Laws were to become barbaric, ensuring that deer would remain the quarry of the nobility, for only the noble and the high born were allowed to own greyhounds. Even a free man who had the guts to run the feudal gauntlet for a year and a day was allowed to keep only one if he lived at least ten miles from the forest.

Exceptions could be made, however, for the Normans were sometimes reasonable men. Such a dog could be kept by a free man living within the forest provided the dog's feet were smashed with mallets, or two of its large toes were severed with chisel blades. Should a free man not allow his beloved dog to be so hacked and mutilated, then special courts were set up to enforce the law, courts that passed decisions against which there was no appeal. All this took place in a country which led the world in its legal system, so that foreign kings came to England to have their cases judged fairly. One law for the rich, another decidedly different for the poor, and all fines collected from free men who had not crippled their greyhounds went to the king. Monks, who came under the jurisdiction of ecclesiastical courts, were exempt from such rules and were openly ready to thumb their noses at the king, keeping uncrippled, unmaimed dogs for sport on the land around the monastery. Chaucer makes mention of a monk who 'greyhounds he had swift as a fowl in flight'.

The clergy were, in fact, great greyhound addicts, and one of the best pieces of advice in choosing a greyhound comes from the Abbess Juliana Berners in her famous *Boke of St Albans*. The Abbess Juliana Berners was more concerned with hawks and dogs than the upkeep of her crumbling manor at Sopwell. Advice she gives, however, rich in rhyme and reason, and as good now as it was then.

> A greyhound should be headed like a snake
> Necked like a drake
> Backed like a beam
> Sided like a bream
> Footed like a cat
> Tailed like a rat.

Good advice in choosing a greyhound, and excellent advice in the choosing of a lurcher, as we shall see later on.

By Elizabeth's reign, however, two types of dog had emerged from the native British greyhound stock. One was a heavier, rough-coated dog used for coursing deer, and the other a smooth-coated dog, smaller in size and more lightly built, more at home pursuing hare than deer. The bigger beasts in time became absorbed into wolfhound types to emerge as the Scottish deerhound, but further changes were to follow to make the divergence of the two types even more noticeable.

Lord Orford, an illustrious name in the field of coursing, came up with a wild brainwave that was to alter the shape and character of the greyhound once and for all. In the 1770s, Orford became involved with breeders who kept a particularly strong and tenacious strain of bulldog. These bulldogs were largely of the type used for pit fighting rather than bull baiting, and they resembled quite lightly built modern Staffordshire bull terriers. Their courage was legendary, their stamina bottomless, for several fights (more grappling matches than fights) went on for an hour or more, and no greater test of stamina could be devised. Orford decided on what must have been considered an outlandish experiment: to inculcate some of the bulldog courage into the greyhound of the day so as to breed a dog with the fire and guts to go on even after physical exhaustion had told it to stop. The flesh, though weak, would be fortified by an irrepressible spirit derived from its bulldog ancestry.

His first generation was largely wastage: heavy in bone, gutsy, but far too slow for competitive coursing. His second generation, after mating these dogs back to good-class greyhounds, produced better dogs: lighter, but still possessing a great deal of the spunk of their bulldog ancestor, and Orford without doubt chose that ancestor well. A coursing man and pioneer geneticist rolled into one was Orford. By the fourth generation he was producing such unbeatable progeny as the famous Czarina, never defeated in a course and progenitor of things to come. Many Irish breeders attribute the brindling of a greyhound and the rose ear to Orford's cross, but this is questionable. We can only say that early bulldogs and greyhounds each had similar types of ear. Ears and colour count for nothing in competitive coursing, however, and it was the pluck Orford had introduced into his stock which made his coursing greyhounds unbeatable. In 1776, he organized the Swaffham Coursing Club in an area famous for its strong hares, and thus began competitive coursing. Other clubs, also with Orford's backing, were soon formed, culminating in the famous Altcar Club – the organizers of the Waterloo Cup, the most famous coursing event in the world. A curious man, Orford, of whom it has been said he was obsessed with greyhounds and besotted by coursing.

Of coursing, its rules and laws, there is scarcely room or reason to mention in a book of this kind. Sufficient to say that two greyhounds, one wearing a white collar, the other a red collar, are slipped at a single hare while a judge on horseback awards points, not for the killing of a hare (indeed, only one in ten hares is killed), but for the dog who has contributed most to the course, or perhaps to the capture of a hare. The judge traditionally signals his decision by raising a white or red handkerchief. Winners compete against each other until a final victor emerges. Cruel . . . well, what bloodsport can claim to be kind? But it is baffling to know why coursing should be singled out as a focal point of hatred for anti-bloodsport groups. Coursing is so much under a cloud at the moment that it will undoubtedly be the next field sport to be axed – and axed by people who have never seen it and have a very false impression of the way it is conducted.

Yet we must leave the coursing field and the stars of the leash to eulogize on the stars of the track. Greyhound racing in any organized form is of recent origin. Early contests involving dogs chasing a mechanical hare were staged in 1876, but these were regarded as only a joke or novelty. Not until 1926 did dog racing catch on and become a popular sport. Since the time when the legendary Mick the Miller held sway over his competitors, the racing dog has improved greatly in performance. The Miller was such a legend in his time that the tales told about his speed, prowess and track intelligence became somewhat ridiculous, but such a dog would not have lived with dogs like Patricia's Hope or Yellow Printer, recorded by Edwardes Clarke as the fastest greyhounds ever.

21

Track greyhounds – dams of the author's lurchers.

In spite of popular opinion, the greyhound used for coursing and the track dog are practically the same dog. One still finds track dogs with noted coursing dogs in their pedigree, and Clarke's extremely erudite book, *The Waterloo Cup*, a lifetime's work if only in its compilation of the pedigrees, shows pedigrees of Waterloo Cup winners who had such noted race dogs as Hi There and The Mad Tanist in their almost immediate pedigree.

The show greyhound is a rather different proposition, bred, as it is, from similar stock to the coursing greyhound and his racing counterpart, but bred for beauty, not performance. There is a danger here, and a genetic danger at that. The greyhound is remarkable in as much as it is the only breed not to manifest any inherent defects. Hip dysplasia is unknown, P.R.A. is never encountered, hydrocephalus and cleft palates are unheard of. Not that the Almighty made a perfect animal, mind you, but man tested his greyhound's steel on the anvil of work and the weakly went to the wall, no matter how attractive they were. The show-bred greyhounds, stately as they are – and

22

A show greyhound – magnificent, but of doubtful use to the lurcher breeder.

some are remarkably beautiful – are not tested in the fire of work, and sooner or later exaggeration and deformities are likely to manifest themselves in the breed. Hard work and rigorous culling are therefore necessary to preserve the character of the greyhound, but few show greyhounds are given the chance to prove their mettle. Thus unsound animals, lacking stamina, guts and speed and also determina- tion – all the qualities that Orford strove to produce – could quite easily be used to propagate further progeny, beautiful but useless. I doubt if we have reached this stage yet, as no exaggerations have appeared in the show greyhound. Fifty years from now, however, it may be a very different tale.

Again, I repeat, the greyhound is one of the most perfectly developed dogs, lacking any of the deformities which modern man has bred into most show breeds. He is the perfect starting-point for lurcher breeders, and so readily obtainable that breeders should rejoice at the fact that such a perfect animal is within easy reach to create a useful strain of lurcher.

23

It must seem incredible to the casual observer that the beast that was once the dog of the nobility, the dog no mean man might own according to Canute, can be so easily obtained. A few statistics (deadly word, and death-knell of many a good book) may be of use to the uninitiated to allow them to understand the availability of grey-hounds. First, in 1974, 4,968 racing greyhounds were registered by the National Greyhound Racing Club (N.G.R.C.), and of these only a small number were sold as what might be described as house pets. The rest were sold to people who intended to race them, either on licensed tracks run by the strict rules of the N.G.R.C. (and no stricter or fairer rules exist than those imposed by this club), or to people who maybe kennel their dogs at home and race them on unlicensed tracks, commonly called 'flapping tracks'. Such tracks are a thorn in the flesh of the purist greyhound racer who stands by the estimable rules of the N.G.R.C., for not only do some of the owners of such 'flapping' grey-hounds openly boast of chicanery, enabling them to treat the dog in such a manner that it can be made to run faster or slower than its natural speed, but also 'flapping tracks' do not at the time of writing insist on pedigreed dogs being entered for races. Lurchers have, on occasion, been run at 'flapping tracks', and one or two have achieved remarkably good times.

So let us assume that while, on average, 5,000 greyhounds are registered each year, quite a large number must be bred that are not registered, and while these 'no paper' dogs are not worth much to the prospective buyer, one nevertheless sees such puppies advertised. Let us now push up the figure for the number of greyhound puppies born each year to roughly 5,500 – a conservative estimate at that. Many of these dogs are unsuitable for racing, perhaps because they are what is called, in hunting circles, 'jealous hunters', regarding the bobbing, furry, clockwork hare as their prey alone and fighting the other dogs striving to get to it – and fighters are usually banned from most tracks, even the anything-goes 'flapping tracks' frowning on such dogs. Alternatively, the dogs may refuse to display any interest in the clockwork hare, refusing to course it, or else they race after it in a very casual manner. One noted greyhound trainer once told me that the most stupid greyhounds often make the best racing dogs since their sheer lack of brain prevents them from reasoning that the object they ae pursuing is inanimate. Dogs who refuse to course a clock-work hare often turn out to be first-class rough coursing dogs – 'rough coursing' being a term used by lurchermen to describe non-competitive coursing. I have known several racing failures that have pulled down hare, rabbit, fox and even deer – as one recent conviction for deer poaching will attest. Such dogs are, however, regarded as useless by the greyhound racer, and are either put down or willingly given away.

Furthermore, even a top-class greyhound, the type that appears in front of the TV cameras emerging from the traps at the White City Stadium, is usually finished as a racing dog by the time it is five years of age. Thus many of the 5,000 dogs bred each year are into desperate straits when it comes to finding a permanent home for them before their sixth birthday. Though Licensed Tracks perform an estimable and very good job at finding homes for retired greyhounds, not a few find their way to what is euphemistically called an animal shelter, a canine knackers' yard, where they are put to death – humanely, but nevertheless to death. Taking it a stage further, it must be realized that whereas it is commendable to seek good homes for retired grey-hounds, it is frankly impossible to place 5,000 greyhounds in pet homes each year. Hence the lurcher breeder finds it remarkably easy to obtain greyhounds free of charge, either from the Greyhound Rehabilitation Scheme (which insists that the new owner keeps the dogs in a reasonable standard of hygiene and health and sends inspectors around to ensure that these standards are upheld), or during a visit to a 'flapping track', which will usually result in an offer of a retired bitch whose working-man owner is only too keen to find a home for his ageing ward. Furthermore, the lurcher breeder should not let the word 'retired' worry him unduly when breeding from a greyhound. 'Retired', in greyhound circles, merely means just past its peak, and the dogs are usually in an excellent state of health and perfectly suitable for breeding. A few problems may be encountered in breeding from these animals, but these should not concern the lurcher breeder at this stage, and anyway will be dealt with in a later chapter.

•So, future lurcher breeder, we have dealt with the greyhound not in full, for volumes could and have been written on the subject, but at enough depth to enable you to understand the main ingredient of the typical lurcher. Having discussed and described the greyhound, it is time to consider the breeds used to ameliorate the greyhound to produce the lurcher – breeds that will increase the vitality, stamina, 'get up and go' and sagacity of the offspring.

4 *The Sight Hound Crosses*

Walsh, in his erudite book, *Lurchers and Long Dogs*, makes a distinction between what he described as a 'lurcher' and what he considers to be a 'long dog'. A lurcher, according to Walsh's nomenclature, is a greyhound hybridized with any breed of dog other than a sight hound – a hound that pursues its prey by sight rather than scent – whereas a long dog is a cross between two sight hounds of different breeds. Admirable as such a classification may be, it is archaic and certainly not used today in lurcher circles. An advertisement in *Exchange and Mart*, which is certainly the paper for buying and selling lurchers, that advertised the ubiquitous and inevitably false deerhound/greyhound hybrid as a long dog, would cause raised eyebrows among the average sportsmen and total bewilderment to the lurcher fraternity. The word 'long dog' is so rarely used these days as to have been rendered meaningless. Thus, rightly or wrongly, I propose to classify all greyhound hybrids as lurchers. While I accept Walsh's admirably accurate nomenclature, I will refrain from using it, for in the pages to follow it will cause baffling confusion to the reader and, to be utterly frank, to the writer.

The Deerhound
The deerhound/greyhound hybrid, if the advertisements indicate accurately and correctly, is the most common type of lurcher in existence. Sadly, they rarely are accurate, and most of the dogs sold under this heading are certainly not deerhound hybrids. This is not to say that they are any the worse for their dubious ancestry, for many of them are probably excellent lurchers, but they are rarely true deerhound/greyhound hybrids. Leaving the Trades Description Act and its ramifications behind, however, let us examine the deerhound before considering the merits of the true deerhound/greyhound hybrid.

The deerhound is certainly a very old breed. Its origins are, however, a little less certain. The most popular theory, and the most romantic, is that when the wolf became extinct in Ireland, the huge Irish wolfhound ('equal to two men in battle' *Njal's Saga* called it)

The Scottish Deerhound – perhaps the most intelligent of the sight hounds.

became a little out of place. Its shape, 'twixt that of mastiff and grey-hound, made it a little heavy for deer hunting, and it certainly had limited potential as a coursing dog for pursuing smaller game. Thus it became virtually extinct. By this time, the hunting of deer using fire-arms was becoming a popular practice, and as the firearms were seldom as accurate as the modern rifle, wounded and crippled deer often resulted from their use. Hence a dog was required to track a wounded red deer and to hold it at bay for the hunter to dispatch it. The Irish wolfhound was the obvious choice apart from its cumber-some shape. This was supposedly remedied by adding a good-quality greyhound blood to create a lighter, fleeter dog – as impressive as its Irish ancestor and certainly as valiant. The last British wolf, slain at Glencoe in the eighteenth century, was killed by a deerhound. This was no mean feat for any dog, but the Scottish deerhound, to give it its full title, was fast enough to overtake and hold a wounded stag. (Gipsies and tinkers still refer to the deerhound as the staghound – a

27

misnomer, since the staghound is simply a very heavy dog closely related to the English foxhound.)

Another theory as to its origins is that when greyhound types began to divide up into the powerful, rough-coated variety used for deer and the smaller smoother-coated dog used for hare coursing, the former became known as the deerhound, while the latter became (fortified by Orford's breeding) the greyhound. My own guess is that the truth of origin lies somewhere between the two, with just a dash of a few other breeds added. Early this century, the borzoi blood was added to give the breed greater elegance and coat, while a further addition of greyhound blood was made by some breeders, the greyhound being a far more useful type of dog to use than the borzoi, though not nearly as elegant. I also believe that other breeds were added, certainly not to the detriment of the breed, and I recently had further proof of my theory.

The deerhound, along with the whippet, is the most intelligent of the sight-hunting dogs – a dubious distinction since sight-hunting dogs have a well-earned reputation for being lacking in grey matter. To my reasoning, and I have had the questionable pleasure of training every breed of sight hound, something must have been added to improve the IQ of the deerhound, which, when all is considered, is little more than a rough-coated greyhound. My theory was confirmed by an article that appeared in the 17 August 1978 issue of *Our Dogs*, written in the 'Bearded Collie' column by James G. Logan. He mentions that bearded collies were at one time crossed with deerhounds to produce a leggy hill collie, perhaps most useful over rough terrain. Possibly this deerhound blood was absorbed by the bearded collie, but may not some of the bearded collie blood have been absorbed into the deerhound strains, thereby adding the intelligence so desperately lacking in sight hounds generally?

The late John McCleod, keeper in the Grampians, and an expert on Scottish working breeds – uneducated, scarcely able to write, but with a vast font of knowledge on terriers and hunting dogs generally – once told me that, at the turn of the century, few deerstalkers used the classic deerhound to pursue wounded game, but most had very rangy, shaggy collie types that would do the job considerably better than any pure-blooded deerhounds of the time. Might not these dogs, probably deerhound/collie hybrids anyway, have been mated back into the pure strains of deerhound? Deerhound experts will no doubt loudly disclaim that their dogs have any such plebeian ancestry as the humble collie, but they should ask themselves how the deerhound became probably the brightest and certainly most tractable of the sight hounds, and why it has the best scenting ability of its group.

These qualities could have been produced by the addition of collie blood, but they certainly were not the result of a borzoi or greyhound cross. Supposed origins of many dogs, when checked in the cold light of reason, do not I am afraid bear up to examination.

Enough, however, of origins, or at least of educated guesses as to origins. Let us now consider why the deerhound is crossed with the greyhound to produce a lurcher. The reasons are many. First, the deerhound is rough-coated, and the progeny of the greyhound/deer-hound cross are not only the most glamorous of lurchers, but their coats are weather-resistant and also resistant to thorns and nettles (though frankly they mask very bad barbed-wire wounds). Deer-hounds were also used for tracking stags over rocky ground, so the feet of such a dog need to be much stronger than those of the pure-bred greyhound. This quality is also passed on to the deerhound lurcher. Then, if we examine the thorax (chest) of the deerhound, we find it is quite massive in depth, if not in width, and width of chest is certainly not required in a running dog. The depth means that there is ample space for lungs and heart, and with such enlarged organs, increased stamina is the obvious outcome. Furthermore, the deer-hound has the most highly developed scenting powers in the sight-hound family, and this is similarly inherited by a lurcher derived from a deerhound cross. Hence the reasons why the cross is popular.

On the debit side, however, we must consider the fact that the deer-hound male is roughly 31 inches at the shoulder, so first-cross deer-hound/greyhounds, while obviously most impressive, are usually far too large and cumbersome to give a good account of themselves on the coursing field. Further crossing of deerhound/greyhound lurchers with greyhound does reduce the size, but this, too, has its dis-advantages, as we shall discover later. Then the deerhound is, as I have mentioned, the brightest of the sight-hunting hounds, but such intelligence is only relative to the sight-hound family. When compared with the Alsatian, or, better still, a good working border collie, the deerhound is simply a non-starter in level of intelligence. True, deerhound lurchers are biddable to the extent that they can easily be taught to retrieve, and jumping is second nature to them, but the lurcher breeder of old, who required a lot of his dog – the working of long nets and gate nets, the carrying of the lamp beneath the neck to attract and catch night-squatting partridges – would not have countenanced a deerhound lurcher, however fast and agile these dogs may be. The deerhound lurcher, particularly one with an extra dash of greyhound (that is, deerhound x greyhound x greyhound), is fast, agile, athletic, but hardly a brainy dog when compared to many of the other lurcher types. Also, being a sight-hound-bred lurcher – a long dog by Walsh's definition – the hybrids respond to commands with the irritating slowness so characteristic of their kind. Still, if one requires a good fast hare dog, an athlete, a thing of beauty and, whisper it again in the light of tomorrow's possible legislation, a deer-hunting lurcher, such a hybrid is ideal. From the point of view of intelligence, do not expect too much, however, or you will be bitterly disappointed.

A further comment which should be added is that few of the deer-hound/greyhound hybrids advertised are derived from deerhounds. There are few deerhound breeders in Britain, and fewer still who offer their dogs at public stud to mate to greyhounds with the object of producing a lurcher. Some years ago a close friend of mine, with retirement allowing him to have time on his hands, followed up some fifty-three advertisements for deerhound/greyhound puppies, and found only one litter to be *bona fide* crosses. Nuttall of Clitheroe did at one time breed genuine first-cross dogs, and very handsome ones at that, and he even had a deerhound at public stud to greyhounds, but I know of few others who breed this authentic first cross.

As a sight hound itself, the deerhound is sometimes used as a grey-hound type of base for lurcher crosses. Jimmy Keeling of Liverpool bred an interesting litter of Staffordshire bull terrier/deerhound crosses, too heavy for his liking, but quarrelsome, plucky and able to take on any quarry from fox to red deer. Collie/deerhound crosses were sometimes advertised some years ago, and were probably quite useful, combining the size and speed of the deerhound with the incredible brain of the collie. Pattinson, in his very enjoyable chapter in Standfast Press's *Coursing*, seemed to suggest that such a cross would produce a useful lurcher.

The Saluki

In recent years the greyhound/saluki lurcher has become a very popular cross, particularly in the south of England among coursing men daring or unwise enough to run Salisbury Plain, an area of undulating fields and gunfire, for much of it remains a military train-ing ground. At a recent show which I judged in Guildford, almost a third of the lurchers were saluki/greyhound hybrids. In the light of such a comment, it is therefore necessary to examine why the saluki should be so highly regarded as a producer of coursing lurchers.

The saluki is a sight hound, similar to the greyhound in shape, build and structure. Its head is even more narrow than its greyhound cousin, and its limbs have a most deceptive, fragile, appear-

Salukis – famed for stamina, but very intractable.

ance – very deceptive, if one has ever seen one of these dogs course over rough ground. The greyhound of the desert, early cynologists called this dog, and indeed that is what he is. The best coursing strains are still found among the nomadic tribes who helped Lawrence of Arabia to storm Aqaba. It is undoubtedly an ancient breed. I would go further still and suggest it is perhaps the forerunner of the greyhound. Even more curious is the fact that the greyhound spoken of by Solomon was undoubtedly the saluki, for the desert tribes along the Fertile Crescent have owned these dogs since the days before Joseph was advisor to the Pharaohs of Egypt. The Moslem faith considers the dog to be a filthy creature (*Haram*), but the Arab nomads do not consider the saluki to be a mere dog, allowing it into their tents, and even referring to it as el-Hor, the 'noble one'. Dogs of this type are rarely, if ever, sold, and the first of these dogs to come to Britain were gifts given to British dignitaries by sheikhs who wished to show great gratitude to or respect for their foreign guests.

The staple quarry of the saluki, and of his kin blood, the Afghan

31

hound, which is little more than a very hairy saluki more suited to the hostile climate of Afghanistan, is the gazelle. Normally two salukis are considered to be needed to bring down the gazelle, but one alone can course the fleet desert hare – a species allied to our own brown hare. Jackals are also usually taken by a pair of salukis rather than by a single dog. To train these dogs, the Arab boys run the puppies on jerboa, or desert rats, until they are dextrous enough to deal with rabbits and hares. They are then, and only then, extended to gazelle. It is a commendable training programme, which is possibly why the Arabs have greater success at training this dog than do most British sportsmen. Gazelle are incredibly testing quarry for any sight hound, for not only are they the most fleet of quarry, but their innate fear of man makes them very wary and difficult to approach. Thus a slip at a gazelle has to be a very distant one, or some method must be found to ensure that the dogs are given a reasonable chance of taking their quarry.

To this end the Arabs adopt a practice called chirk hawking. Here goshawks or saker falcons are taken as nestlings and allowed to feed only on strips of meat hanging from the eye-sockets of a stuffed gazelle. As they grow older they are encouraged to jump for the meat and to bind to the head to feed. Once the hawk has been so conditioned to expect meat to be hanging from the eyes of every gazelle, it is taken out and flown at live quarry. Such is the stupidity of the hawk or falcon, for birds of prey occupy a very low rank in the avian intelligentsia, that they repeatedly strike at the head of the fleeing gazelle in the hope of obtaining food. The beast is thus baffled and bewildered by this ariel bombardment, and is then coursed by a pair of salukis. Cruel, perhaps, but what an amazing feat to harness the instincts of a predatory bird and a dog into one very efficient team.

The saluki's construction belies its frail, almost fragile appearance. Its ability to outrun any quarry in a grinding war of attrition is legendary. There is a story among the Harrareet tribe that one famous cream bitch ran a gazelle from sunrise to sunset, her companion courser dying during the heat of the noon. By nightfall the gazelle had died of exhaustion, and its demise was closely followed by that of the dog. An exaggeration, perhaps, but the saluki is famed for its stamina. It has been suggested that the saluki never really extends itself as does the greyhound who burns up his great speed in 800 yards or so, and is then an exhausted mound of flesh. Certainly the saluki's effortless grace does give the impression of not really trying, but stamina it has, and stamina a-plenty. It is a dog capable of one lengthy course after another. Pattinson, in *Coursing*, suggests that the saluki is built purely for work in desert conditions – conditions uncluttered by the fences, gateposts, tree stumps and so forth which are encountered in the English countryside – and that constitutionally it is unable to take the wear and tear which such conditions are bound to impose. There is, perhaps, a hint of truth in this, as many salukis and saluki hybrids tear easily in country where wire is a curse. They seem to suffer badly, but as for their inability to take the bumps and blows of a typical English rough coursing scene, Pattinson could not be more wrong. I have trained – a loose word when one considered the disposition of the dog – three salukis, and have seen each 'come off' a collision with a gate at such a rate that I could hardly believe they would have survived it, yet all three continued their courses apparently unin-jured by the impact. Thus it is fairly obvious why saluki/greyhound hybrids are very popular among the lurcher fraternity, particularly in districts where there are great expanses of open country that test the stamina of a dog to the full. They are very popular around Salisbury Plain, and are bred in great numbers in the Gwent area of South Wales.

Is the saluki therefore apparently the ideal lurcher or long dog? Well, there is invariably a fly in the canine ointment, so I shall be perfectly frank and basic and declare that the saluki is the least intelligent of the sight hounds, tying for this dubious distinction with its hairy cousin, the Afghan, both of which must for structural and psychological reasons be lumped together. Having said that they are the least intelligent of the sight hounds, may I add a rider and state that the sight hounds are the least intelligent members of the canine world – which, on consider-ation, puts the saluki in a very lowly position among the canine intel-ligentsia. Harry Glover, in Standfast's estimable book *Coursing*, in the chapter on the Afghan hound – again, I repeat, merely a hairy-coated saluki – states that these dogs are too intelligent blindly and unques-tionably to obey commands. While such breed loyalty is highly com-mendable, it is also highly unscientific and should be disregarded if the lurcher trainer intends to get beyond square one in his training programme. Tractability must be equated with intelligence, or, in words that my close friends will find familiar, if a dog can be trained it is intelligent, if it is untrainable it is not intelligent.

Sight-hound breeders frequently argue (in support of their beloved pets) that cats are untrainable and are still regarded as intelligent. Quaint, but again horribly inaccurate and very unscientific. To my knowledge, no intelligence tests have yet been devised to test the IQs of cats, but numerous tests have been designed to test those of dogs, and without exception sight hounds, and salukis in particular, come off badly in them. There have, it is true, been people who have trained sight hounds to the somewhat clockwork requirements of the

Kennel Club obedience tests. In response to this, I congratulate them. They must indeed be among the élite and most patient of all dog trainers. Konrad Lorenz probably started the idea that trainability is not necessarily a mark of intelligence in his book *Man Meets Dog*. At the risk of seeming to question one of the most famous names in animal psychology, I am afraid that Lorenz is quite wrong. He is a student of animal behaviour, and he quite openly confesses to not being a dog trainer. Professional dog trainers all equate trainability with intelligence.

Hence the fly in the ointment, and yet another, I'm afraid, is the question of temperament. On certain days salukis will try desperately hard at a course, literally breaking their hearts to come up on their hares. A few days later they will perhaps make only a half-hearted try at the same quarry. For the best part of a year, Brian Broom and I tried to arrive at an answer as to why this should be so. Did factors like weight or weather have anything to do with performance differences? Neither of us could come up with any explanation. Keeling of Liverpool, not a scientist by any means, but a keen and accurate observer of canine behaviour and one for whom I have great respect, once told me that his own salukis would vary in their interest in the chase from day to day. Thus, not only is the saluki low in intelligence, it is also capricious and fickle by nature. The one ray of hope for all those saluki breeders, loyal to the last to their beloved dogs, is that perhaps, and only perhaps, the saluki may be the least understood of all dogs, and tests devised by those who understand their temperament (and surely there must be some who do) might in due course lift them from the bottom rung of the IQ ladder. But we must now move on to the saluki hybrid.

When crossed with greyhounds, the progeny are fast, agile and usually have great stamina. They are none too intelligent, but, curiously, are as a rule brighter than either parent. Perhaps the phenomena known as hybrid vigour has something to do with it – horses and donkeys are not as intelligent as mules. It is difficult to say categorically, but even the hybrid is not exactly gifted with brain power. Most are triers, and all have the saluki stamina to a greater or lesser degree. To summarize, the saluki lurcher is ideal for competitive coursing events such as those becoming popular in Britain today. It is capable of great speed and admirable turning ability, and has great jumping skills, but for the more complicated tasks that the poacher of old required, very few of the saluki hybrids have brain enough to learn them. While some can be taught advanced training, it needs great skill and even greater patience to train such a dog to this standard.

The Irish Wolfhound

This is the largest of the sight hounds, and there have been several specimens which measured a yard at the shoulder. Besides being the tallest of the sight hounds, it is also the heaviest, probably representing one of the links between the true sight-hound groups and mastiffs. These were the dogs of the Irish chieftains: dogs used to hunt wolf, elk and even boar. They were war dogs, fighting alongside their Irish owners, filling the enemy with fear at their size and their ferocity. 'I will give you a dog equal to two men in battle,' said King Myrkjaten to Gunnar Jarl, and it was a dog of this sort that he meant. This was

Irish Wolfhounds.

35

the dog in Irish legend that the boy Séntanta killed in trying to enter the hall of Culain the Smith, who had allowed the great hound to patrol the stockade while the King of Ulster was present there. Majestic, noble and useless once the wolf had become extinct, the wolfhound had to be revived by introducing such allied blood as deerhound, borzoi and Great Dane, and to give the dog the power of the old war dog, mastiff blood was probably also introduced. Thus the resuscitated breed is quite likely more beautiful and majestic than its forebears.

Handsome is as handsome does in the coursing field, however, and the dog is far too big and clumsy to be of use as an all-round coursing dog. True, in other countries they have distinguished themselves against bear, cougar, wolf and even kangaroo – a formidable quarry in spite of its quaint appearance – but such beasts are not to be found wild in Britain, so the Irish giant is totally out of place in coursing British quarry.

Even hybridizing the dog with the greyhound does little to rectify the clumsy qualities. Several may be seen at lurcher shows, but none ever seem to win, for they are far too tall and heavily built for hare coursing. They probably have a use as deer-hunting or fox-killing animals, for their great size and strength puts even the red deer well within their capabilities. Several have distinguished themselves as fox killers. One, in Brecon, has a tremendous reputation as a fox slayer, accounting for 200 in a year. Pattinson, in the lurcher chapter of the book *Coursing*, certainly the most entertaining chapter in the compilation, mentions one such dog, a wolfhound/greyhound lurcher that he purchased in Liverpool which was quite useless at hare coursing, but became a veritable demon to fox.

Yet, as a coursing dog, the wolfhound hybrid remains a non-starter. Furthermore, while it must be admitted that many are good fox killers, so are a great number of lurchers who are also excellent hare- and rabbit-coursing dogs. In fact, any dog above, say, 23 inches at the shoulder, if properly encouraged and properly entered, will take fox reasonably well, and a dog in excess of 30 inches at the shoulder is no better a fox killer for its extra size. Furthermore, the Irish wolfhound is not exactly famed for its intelligence, so the result of hybridizing a greyhound with an Irish wolfhound is a lurcher bereft of speed, agility and, frankly, wits. It is certainly not in the running for the title of 'all-round coursing lurcher'.

The Borzoi

The borzoi is a gaze hound, or sight hound, of Russia, and a synonym for the breed is in fact the Russian wolfhound. The breed was used for

The Borzoi or Russian Wolfhound – elegant but of doubtful use in lurcher breeding.

wolf, deer and even boar hunting, and the smaller, finer-boned specimens were considered suitable for hare coursing. Tolstoy's *War and
Peace* contains a classic account of a hunt using a bobbery team of
beaters, fox hounds and borzois. Elegant and fast, the borzoi is truly a
beautiful animal, its very name meaning fleet or fast.

Here, however, the eulogy ends. The dog shares a common
ancestry with the saluki and possesses the same vices: lack of intelligence, intractability and capriciousness. Add to this the fact that the
borzoi does not have the saluki's reputation for stamina, and towers
above his desert cousin, and the position is obvious. Again, few are
tested by coursing and are bred simply for their looks. This aspect
must not be decried too loudly since few people buy a borzoi to course
hares and such-like, but coursing qualities such as speed, agility and
tenacity are easily lost if the parents of a litter are not thoroughly
tested in the coursing field. One curious point is that most borzoi

enter very quickly to fox and need far less encouragement to tackle this quarry than do other sight hounds. Two dogs purchased from Davidson's Kennels in North Wales live quite near my home, and I have watched both of them course fox with an almost insane fervour – a fervour totally absent when a hare gets up in front of them. Perhaps a race memory of the time when they hunted wolves and similar canine quarry still lies dormant in this breed, unerased by generations of unentered show dogs.

Few people breed borzoi/greyhound hybrids, and for quite obvious reasons. While they are fast, reputedly excellent jumpers and many try very hard at quarry, as coursing dogs and all-round lurchers they are probably inferior to a well-bred coursing greyhound, and certainly are no more intelligent. Should the proud owner of a genuine borzoi/greyhound lurcher consider that I am perhaps being too hard on the cross, may I offer a prize of, say, £100 to the first person who can show me a genuine borzoi/greyhound lurcher that can lamp, gate net, long net and hunt up – all tasks which well-bred lurchers should be able to perform. Furthermore, I would be prepared to pay homage at the shrine of any man who could train such a dog for this task. The elegant head of the borzoi has little in the way of brains and passes little on to its progeny. It is certainly not a lurcher type which I would consider breeding, training or even, owning.

Whippet/Greyhound Crosses

Here is an interesting hybrid lurcher or long dog, bred sometimes for coursing but more often than not as a by-product of track-whippet breeding programmes. After the Second World War, few racing whippet strains still existed and the show strains had little of the fire of the real McCoy racing blood. Other Bedlington terrier, bull terrier and even Irish terrier blood was introduced to revive or resuscitate the old fiery whippet, but a far more successful method was usually to mate a good small racing whippet to greyhounds. Any type of whippet hybrid, provided it does not exceed 32 pounds in weight, can race as a whippet on some tracks, and though the wastage (above 32 pounds) in such litters must be fairly great, some outstandingly good dogs are sometimes produced by this cross – dogs capable of wiping the board with pure-bred whippets when it comes to racing. The wastage, or large dogs above 32 pounds, are usually first-class coursing dogs, having the greyhound's speed and zest and the whippet's incredible agility, being capable of coming off barbed wire and braking at full speed, causing the owner near heart failure but little in the way of vet's fees. Such crosses are common in Yorkshire, where they are known as 'bred-down grews', and also in Southampton, where I

A Whippet – a useful base for lurcher breeding.

am told that dogs from this cross are winning regularly on tracks which do not insist on a pedigree for the whippets and still allow dogs under 32 pounds to compete.

Since writing *Rogues and Running Dogs*, I have discovered that a strain of lurcher bred by mating a large whippet to a saluki is now breeding fairly true to type in South Wales, and that some outstanding coursing dogs are often produced from this family. For straight coursing (not strictly the job of the true lurcher), this cross is probably very useful since whippets are fairly tractable as sight hounds go, and salukis have their incredible stamina. A hybrid 'twixt the two might be quite priceless.

Again I must add that the whippet is a sight hound (I deal with their origins in the separate section on whippet lurchers on pages 00-0) and although its somewhat plebeian background ensures that quite bright dogs were preferred to the more elegant and stupid of the breed, they are still sight hounds, and are therefore not

39

particularly gifted in intelligence. Even so, I must confess, I have seen whippets and whippet hybrids working gate nets and long nets, and even acting as excellent ferreting dogs – 'net guarders' as they are sometimes referred to along the Welsh borders, I believe. Again I must add that it is not easy to train such a cross to a high degree of proficiency, so the would-be owner of a whippet/greyhound hybrid should be prepared to work hard to attain a standard of proficiency, and should also be prepared for some disappointments. It must, I stress again, be remembered that a sight hound of any type is no canine genius and that the amount of work required to train one properly is enormous.

The Pharaoh Hound and Ibizan Hound

Again this is a sight hound of very ancient type – a type hunted by the Egyptians well before Moses led his multitude towards Canaan. It is a relatively new breed in Britain, and is treated as a bit of a novelty by the coursing fraternity. It is a medium-sized coursing dog, around 23 to 25 inches, and not only are they excellent sight hunters, but most

The Pharaoh hound – useful but noisy.

are rumoured to have excellent noses, for the Maltese are reputed to hunt them by night as well as by day. They are also, by reputation, supposed to be quite intelligent, though one should treat this term with care for no sight hound has the brain of a herding or retrieving dog. Intelligence is relative and breeders of sight hounds should realize this before they put pen to paper to give opinions on the brain power of their hounds. Sadly, few do.

As a suitable cross with a greyhound, the Pharaoh hound has some merit. They are fast, strong and hardy dogs, and I have no doubt that useful lurchers will be bred from them. It is a little premature to say how useful they might be, however, as the Pharaoh hound only received recognition in 1968. It is therefore early for any person to make a valid judgement as to their suitability to 'lurcherize'. One point, however, must be made, and a very important point it is, particularly if the would-be lurcherman is a poacher: the Pharaoh hound is a dog bred to give tongue to guide its owner to the quarry. I very much doubt if the average poacher would welcome such a quality in a lurcher. Again, I must confess ignorance about the breed. This is the only sight hound I have not been paid to train, so further comment would unavoidably, be inaccurate.

Of the Ibizan hound, much the same applies as to the Pharaoh hound. They are very closely related, and both have similar tendencies, even down to the quality of giving tongue in pursuit of game.

5 *The Pastoral Breed Crosses*

Pastoral dogs are, quite simply, dogs which are required to work herding goats, sheep, cattle and sometimes pigs or other livestock. They are, with the exception of the maremma (a bit of a mystery, and so rare as to be discounted in a lurcher-breeding programme), the most intelligent of all breeds, and their quiet, subservient nature belies their true character. As I have stated, the herding instinct is, quite simply, a suppressed hunting instinct for driving prey towards the pack leader. The sight of a border collie quivering with excitement, fixing the flock with its 'collie eye' – a mesmerizing device, so Welsh hill shepherds believe – must put the fear of God into any sheep who has the wits to realize the thoughts and sentiments boiling up within the dog. I repeat, herding is hunting instinct only slightly modified. Three anecdotes will illustrate my point far more clearly than could any set of statistics.

In 1976, an outbreak of sheep worrying occurred in central Staffordshire and the slaughter and carnage resembled a battlefield where shrapnel had exploded from a shell. The television news made much of this picture of horror, as did the Ministry of Agriculture, and rightly so, for the damage done in one night amounted to thousands of pounds' worth. The culprits were shot two nights later: an Alsatian and a black and white hill collie – both bored, both denied their herding duties, and hence the herding instinct had degenerated back to one of hunting. The sheep were no longer livestock to be guarded and driven, but prey to be slaughtered.

The second tale is a little more sinister, and if it had reached its logical conclusion the result would have been horrifying. A friend in a village near Lichfield brought back a smart merle and white hill collie from Wales as a present for his four-year-old daughter. The dog had been bred from generations of working dogs, working sheep and sometimes goats. Such dogs can easily be purchased, and fairly cheaply, too, for the Welsh hill farmers are only too eager to unload their surplus stock. The puppy was superbly intelligent but thoroughly unsuitable as a pet. I expressed my opinion as to its

42

unsuitability, but they chose to ignore my advice, particularly after I had asked if I could mate it to a greyhound to produce a lurcher. The family did not realize that the qualities I wished to breed into my lurcher by using their collie were the qualities that rendered it totally unsuitable as a pet, and very dangerous too, as it transpired. The truth of the matter became obvious on his daughter's fifth birthday, when the din and anarchy of a child's birthday party triggered off a chain reaction in the bored collie's brain. The parents had left eleven children in a room for a few moments alone with the collie, and assumed that the screams and yells of the infants must be normal party fun. When the screams grew hysterical, the parents took an interest and, on entering the room, found all the children justly terri-fied, herded into a corner and kept in a group by the snapping of the family pet, who had fixed the 'herd' with its fearsome wall eyes. My friend remarked that the stare was, to use his own words, 'hypnotic', and produced nightmares among the infants for weeks afterwards. It is both alarming and fascinating to speculate on what the conse-quences might have been if the parents had not intervened when they did. Herding had certainly at that moment degenerated into hunting.

My third tale will be more interesting to the canine psychologist than to the bloodthirsty. A few years ago I took a blue greyhound bitch to be mated to a bearded collie owned by the Fosters of Wyre, near Pershore – experts, indeed, on the herding instinct in general and on working bearded collies in particular. As we were engaged in the usual bedlam of mating any greyhound, Mrs Foster's bearded collie bitch herded a small clutch of chicks and a hen repeatedly into the house towards her, pinning them 'twixt the Rayburn and the owner. After several such gathering-up ceremonies had been thwarted by Mrs Foster, I found the collie herding the brood towards my van, which held my greyhound bitch in paroxysms of excitement at the thought of killing the whole clutch. Question? Did she, rejected by Mrs Foster, who declined to kill the brood, then take up the notion that the greyhound might fulfil her requirements, as she certainly would have done? There was something oddly frenzied about the gentle gathering of the clutch of birds, as if the dog would have been delighted to kill them but had been trained and bred to herd rather than slay.

Clearly, you may say, however, the combination of herding blood, sublimated hunting instinct and brain power with the speed of a grey-hound must provide the ideal lurcher. Would that life was so easy! Before indicating the problems that can be encountered in breeding the pastoral/sight hound lurcher, let us deal with the various breeds of pastoral dog that can be used: the Border collie, the bearded collie, the rough or lassie collie and the Alsatian – which it may surprise many people to learn, was bred to work sheep. *Schaeferhund* – sheep dog – is what the Germans call the Alsatian.

The Border Collie

At the time of writing, just as the show craze has barely begun to encompass the breed, the Border collie is still the genius of the canine world. Twenty years from now, when he is bred for looks not brains, ear carriage rather than stamina, and ability to stand motionless before a point-picking judge, this statement may well be no longer true. At the present time the Border collie undoubtedly remains the MENSA representative among dogs. You will need to examine his qualities closely before finding maybe just a tiny fly, a mere midge, in the ointment. Think of a breed specializing in a task – a spaniel, for instance. A Border collie will, and does, retrieve equally well. What of a Labrador? – anything he can do a collie can be taught. It's not fashionable to turn up at a shoot with a collie, but he could do the job. Guide dog for the blind? – well, maybe he is a little bit excitable, but Border collies still do well. Obedience work? – he has no equal.

A 25 inch hill cattle dog – the ideal collie to use for lurcher breeding.

Maybe he is too large to get to ground to fox, but I have seen collies draw badger and kill foxes often enough. Guard dog? – doing a delivery round in Welsh sheep country will dispel any doubts on this score. Nose work? – ask a mountain-rescue man or wartime ARP warden about a collie's ability to distinguish living from dead under an avalanche or pile of rubble. Stamina as compared with the saluki? – well, tests done with gauges attached to the legs of collies show that a hard-working Welsh or Scottish sheepdog will do a hundred miles over rock and heather fell and bog, and sleep, ill-fed, in a rickety outhouse, but be ready to go again at dawn.

By the age of six, most working collies are burned out, old before their time, fit only for a canine knacker's yard, but they will have earned their keep well enough by then, and ten times over if the truth be told. As hardy dogs they are perhaps second only to the Eskimo dogs, but a clear second. I've seen litters reared under cattle-sheds in holes dug out like fox earths and the puppies born in midwinter. Few survive, perhaps, but those which do are hardy, that's for sure. Think of the brightest dog you know, double it, and the answer is a Border collie, hardy, tough, game, equipped with hunting instinct and stamina. Here apparently is *the* dog to mate to a greyhound to emulate or exceed the ability of the Smithfield collie, easily as bright as any drover's dog. Furthermore, as Walsh states in his *Lurchers and Long Dogs*, several strains of collie/greyhound breed nearly true to type. Where, then, is the fly in the ointment? Well, there are two flies actually – microscopic midges, but there right enough. Firstly, a collie of this type rarely exceeds 21 inches, or 22 inches at the most, so the first-cross greyhound/collie produces what is called in lurcher circles a percentage of wastage – that is, of dogs incapable or unsuitable for hare coursing. A high proportion of collie/greyhounds are just a little too small. Many make about 22 inches at the shoulder, large enough, perhaps, for a sight hound to sight-hound lurcher, but not quite big enough for a good all-round lurcher with collie bone. If your dog is big enough, reaching 25 inches at the shoulder, and if you are skilful enough, you will end up with the best and most suitable lurcher. How you tell as a puppy whether he will grow big enough is, however, a problem, and, I confess, one I have yet to solve. But there is the first fly for you.

The second fly will arise from a fault in the trainer rather than in the dog. Ask your collie lurcher to face a lion, and he will usually die trying; but shout at him, and he will wet and foul himself; strike him, kick him, and the day's hunt is ruined. He is not a beginner's dog, I am afraid, though in the hands of the professional or competent trainer he will turn out superbly. A good, leggy greyhound type in the

45

hands of a gentle sort of man is literally unbeatable. He will not have the glamour of a deerhound/greyhound hybrid, but the correct type, properly trained, will put any other breed to shame in the all-round lurcher stakes.

The lurcher I have used for most of the training shots throughout this book is a collie/greyhound, or rather a greyhound/collie, hybrid. At the time of writing, he is nearly six months old, so perhaps an account of his progress will suffice to convince any reader of the ability of the cross.

Diary
Breeding collie bitch, Merle, property of the late Dai Fish, Ammanford. 20 inches at the shoulder, all-round sheep dog, general rat killer and lamper, gate net dog. Sire, brindle greyhound dog, breeding unknown, used on flapping track in South Wales, indifferent ability on track, moderate coursing dog. Six puppies born, five

Merle border collie – note the almost 'hypnotic' collie eye. Dam of blue merle lurcher puppy featured throughout the book.

46

brindle, one merle, which Dai Fish has presented to me as a gift, partly because I live on an itinerant route and lurcher thefts are common. Merle is conspicuous as a colour, uncommon, and easily shows face and ear tattoo markings. It is also a photogenic colour and the dog is to be used for training shots.

8 April 1978. Joe Smith returns with puppy from South Wales. Age roughly four and a half weeks – Dai Fish kept no records.

9, 10 and 11 April. Totally intractable, wets in terror when approached, refuses food, bad diarrhoea, normal for a puppy taken so young.

12 April. Feeding from hand. Interest in rolling ball displayed.

13 April. Interest in, and picking up of fur dummy.

14 April. Return of dummy to hand – link with puppy developing rapidly.

16 April. Retrieving uncongenial objects such as key ring. Comes to name. Diarrhoea ceases.

23 April. Sit, lie and stay on command mastered. Retrieving well when object is thrown. Inability to understand 'fetch' when object left and not seen to fall.

1 May. Sit, lie, stay, 30 minutes. Retrieving object that is hidden from him in house. First public performance in front of photographer with witnesses from Bryants Field Sports of Surbiton.

17 May. Simple jumping and retracing 12 yards to fetch a fallen or left object. Sit, lie, stay, 26 minutes, distracted by birds.

3 June. Retrieve of dropped object 45 yards. Witnesses, Terry Ahearne and photographer. Tending to creep in from stay position. Must rectify this or it is a serious setback.

21 June. Photographed by Japanese press. Jumping through gate, retrieving 570 yards to a dropped object. Introduced a dead squirrel instead of dummy. The dog went and hid, terrified of the squirrel.

22 June. Retrieving dead squirrel after much coaxing and play. Returning 624 paces to fetch dead squirrel. Broke to ferret, again terror – jill ferret savaged him. Not a good start, but learnt lesson as to their ability.

29 June. First half-mile retrieve of dead rabbit, excited by rabbit but very gentle. Loses interest in retrieving dummy a little. Frantic for the dead rabbit.

17 July. First paced mile retrieved. Photographed and witnessed by two men from Farnham, Hants. Jumping 2 feet 8 inches with ease.

25 July. Badly savaged by Vampire, my Jack Russell stud dog. Veterinary treatment. He will certainly go back.

17 August. Resumed training, slight limp, return to basic obedience. Some doubt if he will be crippled by Vampire's wounds.

24 August. Limp disappears. Terry Ahearne and I begin serious jumping. Merle, as the puppy is now called, cleared 5 feet 4 inches with rabbit in mouth. Barrier fell, frightening him badly and he refused the second jump.

27 August. Terry Ahearne and photographer. Retrieved 860 yards on dead rabbit dropped unseen. Jumped 5 feet 4 inches with rabbit in mouth repeatedly.

28 August. Found and retrieved alive, tiny diseased myxamatosized rabbit which died on the retrieve.

28 August. Press and photographer. Retrieve of dropped object of over a mile. Jumped 5 feet 6 inches with rabbit. Jump 'through' and 'over' now completely understood. Height 20½ inches, weight 46 pounds – he will be unsuitable for competitive coursing, will start net training in September or October. His sister, equally well advanced mentally, is now 22 inches in height and still has 'knuckle' to grow out. Clearly mine was the wrong choice for the all-round lurcher, but will certainly lamp and learn complex net work.

One point before leaving the subject of this very useful first cross. Three types of Border collie look like emerging in the next few years: (a) the obedience type of collie, trained to perform the very stereo-typed actions required by obedience tests; (b) the sheepherding collie; and (c) the show collie, as yet unspoilt, but time will almost certainly and sadly rectify this. Many of the obedience collies show decided gun-dog ears, possibly because of spaniel ancestry – a photograph in Iris Combes's excellent book, *Border Collies*, indicates such a dog The sheepherding strains, still used for the task for which they were intended, on the other hand retain their wolf-like head and stance. Of the two, my choice for use as a lurcher base would be the sheep-herding dog, whose intelligence allows it to cope with unforeseen circumstances and difficult situations; and while the obedience strains perform with guardsmen-like precision, their performances are rather mindless and stereotyped. Furthermore, a hill collie used for sheepherding tasks will take well to obedience work, but I should like

A very useful border collie/greyhound hybrid.

to see the obedience dog perform the task for which a collie is really intended.

Regarding the improvement of the performance of the first-cross collie/greyhound, a further mating of the collie/greyhound with another greyhound produces a very much faster dog with little or no litter wastage. Whether or not the addition of further greyhound blood reduces the stamina of the dog is open to question, and, of course, the addition of further sight-hound blood does nothing to increase the intelligence of the second generation.

There are very few legitimate breeders of this cross who keep records. I hope to be one shortly, but David James of Walsall has already bred several of this cross and declares that there is little or no decrease in the intelligence level of the progeny through the addition of further greyhound blood. Other breeders of the collie x greyhound x greyhound hybrid confirm his opinion. James's dogs are certainly athletic. They hunt up and try very hard at courses. They are also most tractable, though I would question whether they are as tractable as the first-cross collie/greyhound hybrid. Pattinson suggests that the

49

Collie greyhound hybrids belonging to David James: a variable bunch of lurchers of similar breeding.

collie/greyhound wastage could be minimized by the use of a very leggy hill collie of the type found in Devon which is used more for cattle work than for sheep. It is certainly true that they are taller than the average Border collie, but whether they are of the same intelligence is questionable, and whether or not they are of closely similar temperament is even more so.

Iris Combes in *Border Collies*, shows several prints of various collies, some of which were famed for their ferocity in turning rams and so forth. The Dorset collie was noted for its ability to deal with the truculent Dorset sheep, while the Welsh blue – a slate-grey collie that occasionally appears in litters of trial dogs – was originally bred to cope with the aggressive half-wild goats that lived in Snowdonia. These types should not concern the lurcher breeder too much, but it is interesting that Joe Smith of Halifax, whose dogs I obedience train,

The collie × greyhound × greyhound hybrid – one of the most versatile lurchers.

has been producing a slate-grey lurcher by mating a blue greyhound to one of Mrs Peggy Lytton's collies which carries this slate factor. Colour is unimportant, however. Sufficient to say that a pied collie/greyhound changed hands at Appleby Fair in 1978 for £3,200 – said to be a record sum for such a dog.

The Bearded Collie

The bearded collie is simply an offshoot of the Border collie, and many early bearded collies in fact produced Border collie type puppies in their litters. As a result of this affinity with the Border collie, much can be said for the working bearded collie's intelligence. However, the show bug and the craze for exaggeration has altered the beardie considerably, and the once somewhat shaggy-coated collies now resemble miniature old English sheepdogs. Some strains of working beardie do exist, and they are certainly more intelligent than the show types of bearded collie. I found the difference was particularly noticeable when I visited the Fosters of Pershore, who breed both working bearded collies and the more attractive show variety. There is a startlingly sharp difference in the herding instinct between the

Litter 'wastage': a bearded collie greyhound hybrid – unsuitable for all round hunting.

two types, and the working strains are far more easily trained for obedience and herding work.

As to the prospects for lurcher production when mating a bearded collie to a greyhound, I can at least speak from experience as I have bred the cross by mating a blue greyhound bitch to a bearded collie dog, subconsciously, I suppose, to try and re-create the old Norfolk-type lurcher, or a type quite similar. Most of the puppies were attractive, all were fairly heavily coated, but almost every one of the eleven in the litter was still a little shapeless and cloddy. They were, perhaps, not as bright as the typical Border collie/greyhound strain I now train, but they learned fairly easily and picked up rudimentary retrieving and obedience. It was, however, the most variable litter I have ever encountered. I believe only one of the eleven went on to become a first-class hare-coursing dog, though all made excellent lamping dogs. Second crosses of bearded collie x greyhound x greyhound may well yield a better, more homogeneous type of dog, though frankly I would much prefer the far less attractive Border collie hybrids. Even so, the progeny of the bearded collie greyhounds all had weatherproof coats and were a great deal more intelligent than the average lurcher to be met around the shows nowadays.

The Rough Collie

The rough collie, or Lassie-type collie, so called from the film *Lassie Come Home* and sundry subsequent and sweetly nauseating series of heart-rending nonsenses (incidentally, the part of Lassie was twice played by a male), is a beautiful animal. Its long, silky coat makes it one of the most beautiful dogs, and its elegant head makes it look far more aristocratic than its Scottish ancestor. Having said all this in its favour, I should add that it is practically brainless and has been ruined by the show craze. The elongated head indicates obvious

A typical dolichocephalic head. The hallmark of a difficult dog to train.

sight-hound crosses which do nothing at all to improve the intelligence of the dog, and the slanting 'oriental' eyes literally reflect the lack of intelligence in the breed. Some years ago, when I was foolish enough to accept shy biters and difficult dogs to train, I undertook the training of several of these rough collies, and to compare their brain-power with the scruffy Border collie is like comparing an educationally subnormal child with an Einstein.

The inclusion of sight-hound blood – denied by most breeders, incidentally, but perfectly obvious when examining the cranial structure – has made the rough-coated collie simply an elegant lurcher type of dog and very little more. In fact, the smooth collie – a cousin of the rough, identical in shape, but lacking the profuse coat – closely resembles a collie/greyhound lurcher. I have seen several rough collie/greyhound hybrids, none of which I found impressive. Nearly all were fleet, for the rough collie itself is a fast dog, but none had the brainpower, the gift of anticipation or the perspicacity of the Border collie/greyhound.

Of course, now and again one will emerge with more notable qualities. Some years ago I heard of a very canny dog bred from a greyhound bitch mated to a rough collie dog that was a renowned hare killer, even in that superb testing ground, Salisbury Plain. It reputedly retrieved well, and could also hunt up, keeping an eye open for the sudden burst of grass that a hare makes leaping away. At the 1978 Guildford Show, I heard many men eulogizing over the ability of this dog, but one swallow does not make a summer and perhaps the animal was indeed a one-off job. The rough collie is certainly not a breed I would recommend as a starting-point for the all-round lurcher.

The Old English Sheepdog

The Old English sheepdog, the bobtail or, as he is now known by the non-sporting fraternity, the Dulux dog, is probably quite an old breed. Once they were reputed to be more gentle than any herding dog, ideal for lambing times and the task of bird herding since their peaceable ways were suitable for avoiding hysteria in poultry on the move. It was formerly a rather gaunt, scruffy beast very useful, very hardy and very tractable. Now, perhaps, the situation is different. The show craze has produced a dog that is extremely long-coated, so long-coated in fact that the eyes are scarcely visible. It is very much a victim of the craze that has ruined nearly all of our breeds. Few are tractable, and to my knowledge none are worked in this country, though I am told by two hunting friends that a strain of bobtail is still worked in New Zealand. It would probably have been a bearded collie type of dog rather than the Old English sheepdog that was the basis for the New Zealand strain. I am frankly not greatly in love with this glamorous though slightly scatty relic of Old England. As a lurcher base to mate to a greyhound, it has something to commend it, though not very much. It produces a lurcher that has a wonderfully weatherproof coat, but most offspring are very cloddy and they certainly cannot hold a candle to the Border collie/greyhound hybrid. Pattinson mentions that he has bred a litter of greyhound/bobtail, and all were heavy, ponderous and not particularly versatile, which must be a decided understatement. Joe Wright of Mobberly, however, bred a litter a few years ago, of which one of the puppies became a very useful dog to my knowledge. I couldn't, however, trace the rest of the litter.

Several crosses of this kind will turn up at shows, all heavy boned, not a quality conducive to rapid take-off and agility during a course. It is not a cross I would recommend, but it is not uncommon to find them bred quite deliberately. Possibly the Old English sheepdog is a dog that many associate with the Smithfield collie, and they mate these heavy giants to greyhounds in the hope of producing something akin to the almost legendary Norfolk lurcher. It is, I should add, a most forlorn hope. The intelligence, fire, courage and stamina of the Smithfield collie were tested in the drover's runs, and nothing of similar ilk is used to test the bobtail.

The Alsatian

This is not a particularly popular cross with the greyhound, for reasons I will discuss later. The Alsatian, being a German shepherd dog, is as a breed very adaptable, like all pastoral dogs so far un-damaged by the show craze. Alsatians have been used with success for many purposes: as police dogs, herding dogs, retrievers and obedience competition dogs, all indicating the dog's versatility. Once they were the traditional guide dog for the blind, and I believe they are still used for this in the United States, though I am told they are losing ground there to the more phlegmatic Labrador.

In spite of its sturdy nature, the Alsatian is a very athletic dog. Crumstone Danko, a rangy male, is reputed to have scrabble-jumped some 16 feet 4 inches, and the police and military put on amazing demonstrations of the jumping ability and perspicacity of the breed. I have known several that worked with a gun quite well, and once trained a white bitch to a very high standard of gun-dog work. Like the Claudian family, the Alsatian family tree also bears two fruits. It has been justly stated that the Alsatian is either the best or the worst of dogs. The number of Alsatians which kill and savage people is alarming, though it may be explained by the fact that the Alsatian is the most popular large dog and hence that more cases of severe Alsatian damage are likely to be reported. Even so, some can be both fearsome and fearful, equal qualities in making a dog dangerous. The aggressive attack out of meanness, and the timid bite in terror, and the effect of either is much the same from a dog weighing a hundred-weight and measuring maybe 27 inches at the shoulder. Shy biters and nervous Alsatians are on the increase, and soundness, such as was found in the first imports, is no longer a characteristic of the breed. Yet the working strains, and there are several, remain excellent all-round dogs and I have had great success in training Alsatians for a variety of tasks.

As a base for a lurcher, the Alsatian is, however, of doubtful value. Most first-cross Alsatian/greyhounds resemble a pure Alsatian in type, but lack the angulation which makes the Alsatian so attractive. Unfortunately, this cross achieved fame or notoriety (much the same thing in poaching circles) through a court case some time back, and I have seen several Alsatian/greyhound litters advertised since then, possibly in the hope of emulating the dubious feats of the dog involved. Its owner had succeeded in using it to kill 180 deer of vary-ing species, including some of the rare and beautiful Père David deer – a wanton slaughter of a deer which has been extinct in the wild for some 3,000 years. This achievement was a mark of shame rather than of virtue: a useful dog used for an ignominious task, so to speak; but whether one admires or dislikes the brutality of such acts, the story does illustrate the versatility of such a dog. Keepers in Germany often use greyhound/Alsatian hybrids for tracking wounded big game in much the same way as the Scottish deerhound was used. Just occasionally a greyhoundy specimen turns up in the first cross, and these are quite priceless, being also quite rare. As a coursing dog, most first-cross progeny are far too heavy for hare hunting, but are very tractable, so litter wastage, though high from the point of the production of hare-coursing dogs, is reduced by the versatility of the hybrid, which can make a useful fox, deer or lamp dog.

56

6 *The Terrier Crosses*

Greyhounds are often hybridized with large terrier types to produce lurchers, the object of the cross being to introduce some of the do-or-die nature of the terrier to produce a valiant-unto-death type of lurcher, impervious to pain, capable of carrying on after the chips are down or the game appears to be lost. It is not a new idea, for, after all, Lord Orford introduced bulldog blood for precisely the same reasons and succeeded in producing the faultless Czarina in a few generations. Terriers are by nature the gamest of dogs, and the terriers most commonly crossed with greyhounds are dogs too large for fox and bred primarily for either pit fighting or badger digging, or both. Further qualifications for courage need not be asked, since both sports require a very game type of animal. In order of popularity, the terriers used to cross with greyhounds are the Bedlington, the bull terrier, the Airedale, the Irish and the Kerry, all of which are not only still hunted by many, but are also, to be perfectly frank, still fought by those who delight in the pointless torture involved in dog fighting.

The Bedlington Terrier

To begin with, the Bedlington terrier is a bit of an enigma. Originally it derived from the same sort of stock as the Dandie Dinmont, called by Winch 'the *crème de la crème*' of all working terriers. The common stock was reputedly bred by tinker families like the Faas and the Jeffersons, who not only fought their terriers, but produced among their own kind bare-knuckle pugilists game enough, though not able enough, to tackle Joe Berks, the awful fighting butcher, who ate a whole turkey at a sitting, then ran a race of a hundred yards after the session, beating all competitors, before fighting the famous Hen Pearce – Joe Berks, breeder of bull terriers, glutton, brawler and ruffian, who distinguished himself by dying a noisy but valiant death in the Peninsular War. He fought both Jeffersons and Faas, for fighting men kept fighting dogs in those days, and as the bull terrier was the hallmark of the London pugilist, so was the Bedlington the insignia of the northern battler. Gipsies and tinkers kept these dogs not merely for fighting, but also for the sports of badger digging, fox hunting and otter hunting, for during the Peninsular Wars the otter became very popular fur in the fickle market of the world fashion.

Some authorities state that the terriers were used to run down rabbit, but this is doubtful, for the older type, the common stock of both the Dandie Dinmont and the Bedlington, lay half-way between the modern types – variable perhaps, but certainly not swift enough to take a healthy rabbit. Courage was the quality for which this stock was noted: a courage so famous that the breeders of Border, Lakeland and even Sealyham terriers used the blood in their dogs, outcrossing with the self-same blood every few generations to keep up the pluck in their strains. Stories of Bedlingtons and their kin blood abound, and I have dwelt on them at some length in my earlier book, *Rogues and Running Dogs*. Sufficient to say that the divergence of type between the Bedlington and the Dandie Dinmont occurred when showing terriers became popular. Oddly enough, the show bug that ruined so many noble breeds originated in the north and spread south, rather like cholera in my view. By the turn of the century, whippet, or small greyhound blood was used to give the Bedlington its present roach-back shape, and the Dandie became more squat than its ancestors. Divergence of type, yes, but the Bedlington continues to be a valiant little battler, used for fox and badger still among the borrans of the North and mated with native terriers along the Welsh border to this day. The Chapmans of Gwent used this blood to produce some game and enthusiastic mink-hunting dogs, as much at home in water as on land. The looks of a lamb and the courage of a lion was the epigram used by Edwardian writers to describe this dog.

As to its merits as a producer of lurcher, the popularity of the Bedlington lurcher should be proof enough for anyone. Phil Drabble, in *Pedigree Unknown*, says the Bedlington is more suitable for crossing with whippets to produce a nimble hedger ferreter, and maybe a lamping dog, but this is not so. Bedlington/greyhound crosses still fetch very high prices in *Exchange and Mart*, and lurcher breeders are frequently asked for such hybrids by travelling men. In fact, a litter of Bedlington/greyhounds advertised in *Exchange and Mart* will invariably be sold before the weekend, usually to tinkers and gipsy folk. Pattinson eulogizes on the cross in his article in *Coursing*, and few people who have owned them want any other type after they have owned and worked a Bedlington/greyhound lurcher.

One peculiarity of the first cross is its odd rolling gait, so often confused with an apathetic movement by lurcher judges. Such a gait, far from indicating apathy, is capable of galvanizing the beast into action at a moment's notice. For appearance, the Bedlington cross varies little from litter to litter. Most have a linty coat derived from their terrier ancestor, to the liking of some (though personally I consider it unattractive, for I find such a dog looks scruffy). But looks have little to do with performance in the hunting field.

Oddly enough, there is little variation in the size of the progeny, so there is little litter wastage. Most of the first-cross Bedlington/grey-hounds level out at 22 to 24 inches at the shoulder, an ideal size for an all-round coursing dog, particularly since both parents are fine-boned, and cobby dogs are unknown in such hybrids. Colours vary from smoke-blue to fawn, and in both coat and type the cross seems fairly homogeneous. It is of interest to note that a group was once formed to discuss the creation of a pure breeding lurcher, using Bedlington and greyhound blood. Interbreeding between first crosses produced some hideous animals, and some of the nearly pure greyhound type, but very few of the typy specimens of the first generation.

So much for looks. Now for performance. Many renowned hare coursers are agile and nimble enough to turn on a sixpence, and are dauntless in courage. During the 1977–8 winter, when fox pelts rocketed to £15 a piece in prime, a team of hunters from the Welsh mining valleys took a huge toll of foxes by lamping them and coursing the foxes with their Bedlington/greyhound crosses. Profitable, but a bit unsporting, since most of the foxes were poached and many South Welsh foxhound packs had a dead season as a result of these hunters. (Eddie Chapman, the terrier man for the Monmouthshire Hunt, says he will breathe a sigh of relief when the bottom drops out of the market for fox pelts.) Such dogs are also capable of taking roe deer, and a pair will find little difficulty in holding a fallow buck. The carn-age caused on a Midland deer park in 1977 was perpetrated by a pair of Bedlington/greyhounds. The papers, who labelled the slaughter with the apt if ironic caption, 'Men Who Give Poachers a Bad Name', showed many deer disembowelled by the dogs, who were not quite powerful enough to finish their quarry. It was this wanton and exces-sive butchering that has prompted members of the Deer Preservation Society to lobby Parliament to introduce harsh laws to prevent deer poaching. By the time this book is published, that Act might well be a reality, not merely wishful thinking by enraged members of the Deer Society.

Bedlington/greyhound lurchers usually make renowned lamping dogs, being nimble enough and having stamina enough for a really hard night's sport. This is certainly the most popular first cross among lamping men in the industrial North. The linty coat and thick skin of the progeny give good protection from all cover and thorns, and make stitching wounds caused by barbed wire somewhat easier than stitching wounds in greyhound or whippet types of beast. Lamping puts a tremendous strain on a dog, who is required to make maybe eighty or ninety courses in a night, and it is here that the terrier stamina and pluck helps the Bedlington terrier/greyhound hybrid to survive.

Faults? Two, perhaps, will suffice. There is no lack of nose in the Bedlington, for this is one of the best scent hunters in the game, but it has to be said that many are very hard-mouthed. Terriers usually are, anyway, since their job involves tackling quarry and this is not a task that encourages a soft mouth in a dog. Secondly, there is the IQ factor, and since terriers are doers rather than thinkers, obedience and advanced training (particularly livestock breaking) can be a lengthy business. Even so, I have seen Bedlington crosses work gate nets, and most are fairly versatile when it comes to ferret work, but it would be foolish to expect the same rapid learning that can be found in a dog with pastoral origins. Bedlingtons are terriers, not collies.

The Bull Terrier

Like the Bedlington, the bull terrier has been used for dog fighting, but unlike the Bedlington, it has been used for little else. A hundred years ago, they were the mark of a man of low calibre, a thug, prize-fighters' dogs. Today they are a fashionable breed. The Staffordshire (as distinct from the English bull terrier) was the real old fighting dog, bred from a judicious and bloody blend of bulldog and terrier, mainly bulldog (the same stuff as Orford used to breed his new type of greyhound), with a subtle hint of terrier. There was just enough of the latter to make it agile – agile enough to get a hold on its foe, the bulldog blood doing the rest.

The bull terrier's courage is legendary, and most are totally impervious to pain. My earliest memory of one is seeing a great pied brindle dog, victor of a hundred village canine battles, knocked down by a pre-war Austin, and come up savaging the wheels. When he is locked on his foe, he grips; hurt him, and he grips harder, taking out his hatred on whatever is between his teeth. So impervious to pain was the bull terrier, that old dog books assumed that his brain was a little sub-standard. Curiously, however, he is among the most intelligent of terriers, though that is, perhaps, a somewhat dubious distinction. A hundred years ago, he was fought against dogs, blinded bears and even men, and although the show breeder has maybe knocked out of him a little of the unnecessary fire, the nuisance kind of spunk, he is still a heller if roused. In 1968 a collie annoyed a noted show Stafford by its persistent harassment, and the bull terrier

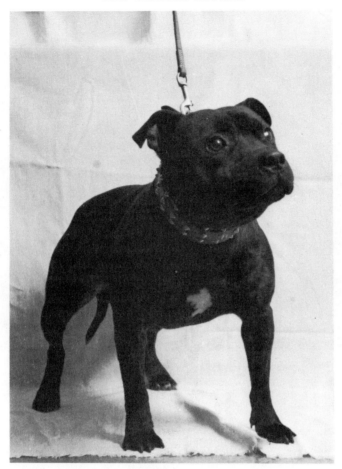

Staffordshire Bull Terrier.

promptly severed the collie's leg. Such a beast is the Staffordshire bull terrier.

The Staffordshire bull terrier/greyhound lurcher is quite popular among the Welsh borders and into North Wales, and its popularity is perhaps justified. The lurchers bred from such parents are usually extremely valiant, fearless of any quarry, and with the guts and determination to run well beyond normal endurance levels. This type of lurcher is commonly used by poachers along the Shropshire border for taking deer. The dogs' pluck and determination are usually sufficient to carry them through the hardest night's lamping and

61

Bull terrier × greyhound hybrid – a powerful head is produced through this mating.

leave them ready for more sport after a day's rest. The lighter specimens make superb coursing dogs, but herein lies the snag, for few are
light enough to be of use as all-round lurchers.

Litter wastage among such dogs is very high. Many of the progeny
resemble small Great Danes or ill-built mastiffs. Breeders who have
used this cross are usually quite content if a fifth of the progeny is
lightly built enough to make coursing dogs, for the ones that do make
the grade are usually superb. Such wastage stock is perhaps a useful
genetic pool for courage and endurance, and further crossing with
greyhounds often breeds out the coarseness in the second generation.
Another potential problem is that lurchers of this breeding may be
only slightly more intelligent than pure-bred greyhounds, and
although they learn the techniques of lamping well enough, the finer
arts that can be so easily taught to a pastoral/greyhound hybrid are
very difficult to teach to a lurcher of this breeding.

Fighting can also be a problem. Keeling of Liverpool once
produced two astonishingly good bull terrier/deerhound puppies:

heavy, but stamina-packed. Both were lethal fighters, and Keeling, I believe, separated them for that reason. He once told me that both would lamp all night and remain literally tireless, but that skirmishes between them were very ferocious. This fighting, the result of introducing bull terrier blood into sight hounds, was also experienced by Walsall whippet racers who crossed a noted red bull terrier from Willenhall into their racing whippets. Even with fourth-generation progeny, fighting remained very bad at the end of races. This is a bit of a problem if one has to kennel dogs together, and it should be taken into consideration before one contemplates breeding this cross. With sheer guts more often than not goes a tendency to fight.

Kerry Blue and Irish Terriers

I have lumped these breeds together, for not only do they share a common origin and similar shape, but both are of similar disposition. Each is aggressive, as are most terriers, but the Irish breeds of terrier have two things in common: all are far too big for the task of getting to ground to fox, which is the real task of the terrier, and all are highly aggressive towards other dogs. As a pro to balance most of the cons,

Kerry Blue Terrier. An uncommon but attractive lurcher can be produced by mating a Kerry Blue Terrier with a greyhound.
(Photo Anne Roslin-Williams)

Irish Terrier. A breed sometimes hybridized with both whippets and greyhounds to breed a particularly valiant type of lurcher.

(Photo Monty)

each breed is highly versatile and they probably comprise the intelligentsia of the terrier world. Dogs of these types are still used for badger baiting, badger digging and even dog fighting in the remote districts of Ireland. That is surely a little far-fetched, the reader may proclaim, since dog fighting was made illegal in 1835. It has to be pointed out that stealing and murder were listed as offences in the legal code of Hammurabi, and they still continue.

As to the usefulness of the progeny obtained from breeding lurchers by crossing these breeds with greyhounds, I have had mixed reports. Since the publication of *Rogues and Running Dogs*, I have received several letters from people who have bred both Kerry Blue terrier/greyhounds and Irish terrier/greyhound litters, all of whom extol the virtues of the hybrids, but all of whom confess that there was great litter wastage. They made useful lamping dogs, perhaps, but most of the progeny were unsuitable for coursing dogs.

The Airedale

This, as the largest of the terriers, is far too big to get to ground and was bred originally for ratting in the rivers of North Yorkshire. It is believed that the breed was the result of crossing otterhounds with pit-fighting dogs. Lucas, in his book *Hunt and Working Terriers*, goes as far as mentioning the names of the parents of the breed and the date

*The Airedale. A breed sometimes crossed with greyhounds to breed a
'gutsy' lurcher.*

of the cross, but both pieces of information can be discounted as nonsense. To refine the hideous specimens bred in the early days, Irish
blood has been added and the Airedale now resembles a very large
Welsh terrier. Most have excellent noses and, despite their
fighting-dog origins, are fairly placid animals.

Some wastage occurs when mated to a greyhound, but a few
first-class dogs are bred – gutsy, with nose and power enough to suit
anyone. I have judged a few of these crosses in South Wales, and they
are most attractive dogs. This cross is sometimes bred in the United
States to deal with coyote, fox and hare, and has shown itself very
successful at the task. Obviously, with its large proportion of terrier
ancestry, the resultant lurcher is often hard-mouthed, but this in my
view can be as much a result of mistraining as of breeding.

7 Sundry Other Crosses

Foxhound and Beagle Crosses

Foxhound and beagle lurchers are sometimes seen advertised, and are apparently quite plucky. As a legacy of their scent-hunting ancestors, they have acquired great stamina, but on level of intelligence they fall very low. However, they certainly hunt up and course well enough. Simpson's book, *Rebecca the Lurcher* will be of interest to anyone who is contemplating such a cross.

The foxhound – a popular lurcher sire since Simpson's book Rebecca the Lurcher.

Retriever Crosses

Why retriever/greyhound hybrids are not more common than they are is rather baffling. Both the Labrador and the golden retriever are bright, easily taught and very versatile, having good noses and excellent hunting instinct. Pattinson believes that Labrador/greyhound crosses are either very good or very bad. I can vouch for the fact that all retriever bred lurchers are easy to train, and although there is some little wastage through using this cross, the progeny are far more versatile, tractable and useful than most lurchers.

Some thirty years ago, the retriever/greyhound was a common cross to produce the ideal poaching dog, particularly in the Fen country where their ability to take to water made them all-round hunting dogs. I know of an excellent lamping dog, a golden retriever/greyhound hybrid, that is very soft-mouthed and retrieves both hares and rabbits totally unharmed to hand. Some ten years ago, an advertisement was put in the *Field* by a buyer who wished to purchase several hares to restock land in the South (though the legality of restocking land with hares is an interesting point). Several of these were supplied by the owner of this dog, whose lurcher caught and held live hares without marking them.

I am literally astounded as to why this cross should not be more popular. They are so versatile and can be taught so easily. Might it be that, after all, the lurcher owner of today requires a poor-grade coursing greyhound rather than the adaptable priceless lurchers of old? The cross must vie with the collie/greyhound as the most versatile poacher's dog, lacking only the collie's innate suspicion of strangers, a quality so important in a poaching dog. I question also whether the average lurcherman has the ability to train such a dog. At a show, just after I had finished judging, I recently put this point to the exhibitors, who were very much in disagreement with my hypothesis. As a challenge I asked ten exhibitors to get their dogs merely to 'sit' and 'stay'. Not one was able to do it – rather a tragedy when one considers the versatility of the old-fashioned lurchers.

Whippet Lurchers

I will touch briefly on these lurchers, partly because their small size makes them rather inefficient coursing dogs, and partly because I covered this subject at length in my book *Rogues and Running Dogs*. Whippets are probably bred-down greyhounds, or possibly bred-up Italian greyhounds. Frankly, the latter seems highly unlikely as the whippet was essentially a poor man's greyhound, a pot hunter for the families of the workers in the industrial north, and the Italian

Handsome is as handsome does: Steve Jones' lurcher, an excellent hunter, but with turned out elbows, dropped pasterns and little neck. This dog is a noted hare killer.

greyhound, elegant as it is, would have seemed a little out of place in such a setting amid the terriers and pit bull terriers of the average worker. Thus I believe the whippet to be a result of breeding 'down' a greyhound, by dint, perhaps, of the addition of terrier blood. Modern racing whippets, racing on non-pedigree tracks, certainly have greyhound blood in their veins. (The whippet/greyhound crosses have been dealt with separately on pages 00-0.)

Whippet crosses involving collies, terriers of all sorts, and even more exotic breeds are fairly commonly seen in the under 23-inch classes at shows. Few, if any, are hare-coursing material, being more suitable for exercising and frightening hares than catching them, but most are useful rabbit dogs, capable of the lightning bursts of speed that are necessary to take rabbits feeding near hedgerows. Whippet/Bedlington crosses are the most common and popular of the small lurchers. Neil Davidson of North Wales, who breeds both whippets and Bedlingtons, states that he is snowed under with requests for whippet/Bedlington crosses whenever he advertises them. Whippet lurchers are essentially rabbiting dogs, hedgerow workers, snappers up of feeding bunnies and accoutrements of ferreting men rather than coursing dogs. However, horses for courses, as the saying goes, and some cracking whippet lurchers are to be found, usually better trained than their larger brethren.

This completes our account of the breed hybrids, their various types, their uses and failings. Now for the most important section of the book: the training of these dogs. Even so, if the reader is content with a dog that he can slip on hares and nothing more, then the next few chapters will be superfluous to his requirements. They are highly important to anyone who wants an all-round lurcher, however, and I am pleased to say that such people are still in existence.

8 *The Arts of Training and Entering*

Basic Training

If the reader believes this section is unnecessary, I suggest he goes to any show to watch the pandemonium when a lurcher breaks loose in the show ring, and the spectacle of the embarrassed owner chasing madly after his disobedient dog. I did my apprenticeship, so to speak, with springer spaniels, so perhaps the standard of obedience I require may seem high. Sufficient to say that I obtain it with most dogs. I confess to having failed miserably with salukis, Afghans, chow-chows and Basenjis, but most other breeds are trainable to the level indicated. It is always baffling to me to hear a man with his uncontrolled and uncontrollable lurcher boasting that he is a great poacher. Such a dog, a genuine poacher's dog, requires a great degree of control, and a great deal of work must be put in to obtain that control. Do not scoff at the idea of basic obedience and skip this chapter to get to the meat of the book, as it were. Without basic obedience, your dog is little more than a track greyhound, required and able only to run at anything moving. Do not regard basic obedience as 'tricks', as not really necessary and just a little pointless. 'I'm a half-wild man with a half-wild dog,' one exhibitor boasted to me in Cumbria when his uncontrollable dog hared around the show. I felt he had misnamed his fractions – 'half-witted' would have been more appropriate than 'half-wild' in both dog and man.

Advice: start with a puppy and avoid the going dog or the dog just started. To define the reasons, let us examine human nature and explore the real meaning of advertisements designed to sell supposedly trained dogs. Most of the made or trained dogs are usually eighteen months old and killing hare, deer and fox with regularity. Some are three years of age in the advertisements, but are apparently still superbly trained dogs, capable of performing all the tasks imaginable from killing deer to taking an Open University degree. Prices range from £35 to £80. There are the advertisements – now for the facts.

A dog that is truly trained to such a degree will rarely, if ever, be sold. To teach or train such an animal requires months of steady hard work, several hours a day for several months, so even £80 must put a ridiculously low price on the owner's skills. In any case, to ask the

64,000-dollar question, why should the owner be selling such a paragon: a beast capable of keeping a whole street let alone a family in
game? Most trainers who have taught or trained a dog to the level of
near perfection claimed by the advertisements will be highly reluctant
to part with their dogs. Eric Quimby of Alrewas has faced eviction
orders rather than sell dogs he has trained. And, last but not least, the
lurcher fraternity is aware of who has useful dogs and who has not (an
alarming theft rate of lurchers, alas, attests to this intelligence service),
and any such dog would be bought up, and quickly, from among the
owner's inner circle of friends. Thus few top-class dogs are advertised.

Sadly, the majority of lurchers rarely see only one owner, and a great
number of shiftless people possess these dogs, one week buying a
collie/greyhound and the next selling it to buy an Alsatian. Many are
the dealers who buy and sell lurchers, and a dog passed from hand to
hand rarely gets trained, but certainly acquires a myriad of bad habits.
It is no exaggeration to say that I know of one lurcher owner who has
had upwards of forty dogs in the course of a year, swapping or selling
them at the merest excuse, or at the sight of the tiniest fault, in the
forlorn hope of buying a paragon. But a paragon simply cannot be
bought, and the tragedy is the number of homes the average lurcher
sees in a lifetime, and the tragedy of tragedies is where the poor devil
finds its final resting place. It is no overstatement to say that many
lurchermen use dogs instead of money – a process of barter only made
practicable because the greyhound blood in a dog allows it to change
hands quite readily. Pedigrees, the history of the true crosses, are, of
course, lost along the way, and the lurchers advertised have guessed-at
origins. Therefore avoid the purchase of a 'trained' dog. To buy one is
to display the hallmark of (a) an amateur, unable to train his own, or
(b) a fool willing to part with his money all too readily.

My advice, and it is good advice, is to find an honest breeder who has
good dogs, not a dealer who is simply a pumping station on the pipeline
of lurcher supply, and book a puppy. The choice of breeding is then up
to you. Check that the parents are what you want, and you will have a
reasonable chance of obtaining a puppy of the type you require.
Smooth coat, rough coat, dog, bitch, height can all be a matter of
choice – your choice. But choose a puppy rather than act as a stopping
point in the chain of adult lurchers that continue to circulate in the
country at the moment.

Better still, if you can go to the trouble, get a 'free to a good home'
greyhound bitch and breed your own. One thing is then certain: you
will have the pick of the litter and, furthermore, will know exactly how
the animal you are to train is bred. Not everyone has the facilities to
undertake breeding, but a group of enthusiasts getting together to

71

breed a litter from a greyhound bitch and, say, a genuine deerhound or collie dog would potentially be well on the way to producing a good lurcher. Moreover, the fact that friends have similar dogs of the same age will act as a spur to the trainer to produce a better-trained animal, and he will not be so keen to sell it at the first setback as so many lurchermen do. Few dogs jib during training, but lurcher trainers who jib are a dime a dozen.

So, the puppy is obtained. Now to training. First, we should take a glance at a common piece of 'logic'. Many dog trainers state that a dog ought to be left until six months old before training of any sort begins. Logical? Well, it is about as logical as saying that a child should be twelve before teaching it reading or even table manners. We need a healthy breath of science to compensate for the numerous ridiculous stories told by lurchermen. Dogs left in isolation in kennels away from people do not develop their potential intelligence to the full. In short, dogs need human companionship to develop mentally. To put it

Lead training, tedious but an essential part of training.

another way, dogs kept indoors in a family environment are easier to train than kennelled dogs. This is not just an opinion. Scientific tests have proved this to be correct, and I have dealt with the point at length in my book *The Working Terrier* (1978). Leaving a dog in a kennel for six months before taking him out to train is not only useless but will have a deleterious effect.

Training should begin as soon as the puppy arrives. Start calling it to you by name, making a fuss of it, feeding it whenever it comes to you. A dog that runs off and is difficult to recall can often be brought to you by simply crouching and then calling to it. The change in shape either amuses or baffles the dog, who then comes to investigate. Reward his curiosity, and disobedience will quickly turn into obedience. Even salukis come in fairly quickly to a crouched man calling them.

Lead training can be a burden, particularly if it is left until the dog is six months old. It is best taught on a light lead as soon as the puppy is inoculated, and twelve to fourteen weeks old is about right. If it is left until the dog is older, the process quickly degenerates into a tug-of-war match, an upset dog and a relationship gone awry if not broken. Lead training, particularly of lamping dogs, which are usually run off a slip, is vital. A dog that bucks and rears like a bucking bronco is a damned nuisance anywhere, and is certainly out of place on the hunting field. Train gently and train young is the dictum.

'Sit', 'lie', 'stay' – these commands are important to an all-round hunting dog, though it is astonishing to see how few lurchers will actually obey them. They are not 'tricks', as many ill-informed men call them (probably because they lack the skill to teach such tricks), but are essential qualities in a properly trained dog of any sort. Try ferreting while using a dog who wanders about between holes, causing the rabbit to back and stay in its burrow, and the merits of such training will become obvious. Furthermore, the 'stay' command is often more forceful than a 'come back' command when a dog explodes in pursuit of forbidden livestock. I encountered this problem only four days before writing this section. It is impossible to teach dogs all forbidden livestock, particularly in countryside where exotic fowl are kept. Merle, my collie/greyhound, chanced upon a peahen, and having been taught that pheasants were fair game, naturally gave chase. 'Come back' would not have halted him. 'Stay' did, so I am still allowed on the estate in question.

Thus the merits of training are (or should be) taken as proven. How then to teach these skills? Lead training is essential, for few dogs enjoy sitting, lying, staying and so forth, and most tend to run off when they consider they have had enough. Seven weeks is not too young to start basic training if the puppy is lead trained by then, though until

Sitting training: 'Merle' aged 6 weeks.

inoculation it is unwise to take him out on the leash for exercise. Take him on the lead and gently force down his hindquarters, uttering the 'sit' command quite forcefully, but not enough to frighten him. Ten minutes a day with a puppy this age is enough. More will cause him dismay, and he will not benefit from the experience, but will tend to regard the whole thing as an irksome chore. I once had a five-week-old puppy conditioned to 'sit', 'lie', 'stay', but this was to satisfy my own vanity and is not really necessary at this age.

'Lie' is also easily taught as soon as 'sit' is mastered, and this is done by forcing the forequarters of the sitting dog down as the command is uttered. Any poacher worth his salt and determined to stay out of prison should be able to get his lurcher to 'lie' instantly. After a while, the command can be uttered from a yard or so distant, raising an arm as one utters it. Eventually the dog will drop to command, or even drop to the signal of the raised arm. This is a most vital exercise in training and must not be omitted. It is also regarded as tedious and unpleasant by

74

'Lie' an essential command: 'Merle' aged 6 weeks.

the dog, so should not be overdone. I have every reason to know this since my mistakes in training would fill a book ten times over. Some twelve years ago I trained a Welsh springer spaniel – not as easily disciplined as the English springer – and persisted in the 'stay' and 'lie' lessons long after the dog had had enough. In dog-training terms he 'broke' and ran for home, away from the idiot who was pushing him too hard. On the way for home, he was killed by a car. I learn well, but by mistakes, and costly mistakes. Since that time I have never overdone the 'sitting', 'lying', 'staying' sessions. It is a chore for the dog, and since no dog enjoys doing it, the trainer should allow the animal to indulge in a wild game after every session.

Staying on command is another task no dog enjoys. It is done from 'sit' or 'lie' position, and by uttering the commands 'stay lie', 'stay sit', as one backs away. When one is facing a dog, he is usually easily kept in the staying position, possibly by the gaze of the owner, for staring has a controlling, mesmerizing or frightening effect on dogs (Mowgli was thrown out of the wolf pack because his staring could not be tolerated), staring or prolonged gazing usually being a prelude to attack among animals. Walking away from an animal with one's back to it is another matter, however, and many dogs creep forward. This can be prevented by shouting, 'Stay lie . . . Stay lie,' every few yards while walking away from them.

75

Stock-breaking is another vital part of training, and is best done at this age. A twelve-week-old inoculated puppy can easily be checked from chasing sheep, cattle, cats and chickens, but it is a lot more difficult to break a dog once it is older. A cow, or ewe with a lamb, will fill a puppy with dread, thereby preventing future stock worrying, and it is wise to remember that during a long course the dog is out of your sight for most of the time. A dog that is unsteady with sheep is truly a great worry to anyone who has any sense of responsibility and decency. Early breaking to livestock is absolutely vital. Collie lurchers are very bad stock worriers if they are allowed to be, and pure-bred sight hounds are such a problem that few canine insurance companies will issue the owner of a sight hound with third-party cover against the dog worrying livestock. Sight hounds have been bred for thousands of years to chase any moving creature, and unless your lurcher (who is part, or all, sight hound) is thoroughly stock-broken as a puppy, he will be the problem of problems to you.

Cats are great attractions to lurchers, and many foolish lurchermen boast how many cats their dogs have killed. It is madness to allow this, for not only does a cat stand a good chance of selling even one of its lives quite dearly by blinding your dog, but cat-worrying dogs are not especially welcome on farms where cats abound – unloved, of course, but the killing of them is not really appreciated. Furthermore, farmers who see your lurcher worrying cats will have doubts as to what he will get up to at lambing time! Stop cat-worrying by allowing a fierce old tom or queen to give your puppy a swipe or two, painful perhaps, but certainly better than the blindness that so frequently follows the killing of a cat. Men have been killed by attacking cats, and a lacerated dog and an irate cat owner are the only prizes for killing a cat.

Once we have a puppy that is stock-broken, obedient to 'sit', 'lie', and 'stay' commands, we pass to the most important and often neglected part of advanced training: namely, retrieving – and few hounds retrieve by nature, preferring to stand over their kill. Therefore I will dwell at some length on the art of teaching retrieving – and, reader, an art it is.

Retrieving

In my forty years I have been on the receiving end of perhaps two good pieces of advice – not a lot for nearly half a century on this earth. The first, given me by my mother, was, 'Forget about dogs and ferrets and such-like, or you'll not get on in this world.' The second was given me by Tom Evans, the famous springer breeder: 'You can thrash any part of training into a dog if you have to, but retrieving has to be a game.'

Both pieces of advice have proved true. Interest in dogs has prevented any progress of mine in the teaching profession, and retrieving is certainly best taught as a game. Come to think of it, I've valued Tom's advice far more than my mother's forever negative piece of wisdom.

The point to make at the outset is that chasing and killing game is a very natural instinct in the sight hound while retrieving is not. The introduction of blood other than sight-hound blood does increase the propensity for retrieving, but the reader would be surprised how many lurchers do not retrieve. It is a fault in training that causes this, and provided retrieving is taught quite young, it is easily learned and permanently remembered.

Retrieving, then, has to be a game, and the more exciting the game the better it is when starting a puppy to retrieve. It has to start as a game of wild abandonment, and only after the technique has been learned, and learned well, should any restraint be taught. As soon as

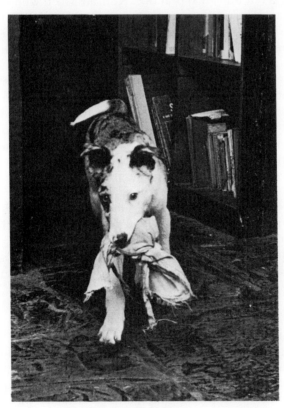

Early retrieving training is essential. The author's 'Merle'
at 6 weeks of age.

77

any tedium or disinterest is displayed, the game should stop, and stop immediately. Make retrieving even slightly a chore, and you are truly lost. There was a philosopher and educationalist, and a wise one at that, called William James, who said, 'The essential difference between play and work lies not in the nature of the activity itself, but in the attitude of the doer towards it.' He would have made an excellent dog trainer. Retrieving is an essential part of the lurcher's work, but it must be made to seem to him like a game. Enough of philosophy, and so to work. How do we start?

Again the answer is as soon as you get the puppy. Forget dog-training manuals that state 'wait until six months old before starting retrieving' – unscientific and time-wasting. Training of this type or nature can start as soon as a puppy is weaned, or, indeed, as soon as a puppy can focus its eyes on an object more than two or three feet away. I start training indoors away from the distractions of the outside world, though this is not universal practice. Konrad Most, who was in charge of war-dog training in Germany, and whose ideas I will discuss later, believes that 'drawing-room training' has a deleterious effect. Even so, I start in the house. First, a small, light object that can roll is shown to the puppy and rolled away from him slowly. He is held until its movement excites him to near frenzy. When he is really excited, he is released and will invariably pick up the object. Crouch immediately and make a fuss of him and allow him to return it to you. Easily done, but don't do it too often – stop while the dog is still regarding it as a game. This works well with most dogs, and praise of a verbal kind is the added incentive. At one time I used to give scraps of meat as a reward when the dog retrieved the ball or dummy, but puppies trained in this manner usually find the meat in your bag more interesting than the rolling object. They tend to poke around the food instead of pursuing the ball. Praise first and maybe food rewards later are the priorities during the more complex retrieving training.

Maybe this method will fail with your dog. Well, he is sight-hound bred and training sight hounds is always a bit more difficult than the training of spaniels or labradors. He perhaps shows total disinterest in the rolling ball and merely walks up, sniffs it and returns. You are still not beaten. There are other ways, so forbear from placing a 'puppy for sale' advertisement and persevere.

Your dog is a sight hound, a chaser of ground game, furred game, therefore harness his instinct. Make your dummy of fur, preferably using a rabbit skin but a fur glove will suffice. Next prepare to look foolish in front of your friends and relatives. Attach a piece of string to the dummy, dragging it round the floor in front of your puppy. He will almost certainly chase it. To start with, jerk it out of his way, generate excitement, encourage him to become almost ecstatic about the dummy. The whole affair must build up into an almost insane game. When he is really excited, allow him to catch the fleeing dummy. He will almost certainly grab at it and bite it. Now throw the dummy and string, allowing him to catch it. Crouch and encourage him to come to you. Praise his efforts almost madly, allowing licking, jumping and petting (hygienists may flinch at the licking, but psychologically it is simply a sign that your puppy acknowledges your supremacy, a sort of 'Hello boss' response). Again throw the dummy. Again accept it, and then quite suddenly, while the game is still hot, place the dummy out of reach and stop the game. Do not be encouraged by the pleading glances from the puppy. It is fatal to overdo the training at this age. Throw once too often and you will be back to square one.

The next day allow him to play again until he is very excited, and then once more stop the game when he is near fever pitch. Let him see you place the dummy out of reach. Sooner or later, depending on the breeding of your dog, he will begin the training session by whining at the spot where you have hidden the dummy. You are now winning, hands down. He is at least over stage one of the programme of retrieving. Again, I repeat, it must remain a game, it must be stopped before it becomes tedious, it must be rewarded with excited fussing. Excitement, like fear, is an infectious feeling 'twixt man and dog.

But now let us assume you have not heeded any advice, have bought a grown dog and seen the error of your ways. He was, of course, originally trained by expert lurchermen. He has known a dozen homes, failed a dozen amateur trainers and now he is yours. Even so, he can still be trained, though it may be to forced retrieving methods that you will have to turn, rather than to the simpler 'game' methods described above. Let me first explain the principle of forced retrieving, the greatest all-time exponent of which was Colonel Konrad Most of the German Military Dog Training School; though it must be emphasized that his techniques are frowned on in the dog world and are illegal in Britain. They also work well on difficult and violent dogs, but leave a timid collie type of dog a cringing wreck. His methods must be explained, however, and it must be stressed that Most took difficult, vicious and untrainable dogs and made useful animals out of beasts that were well on their way to canine condemned cells.

The techniques were founded on a theory that a dog avoids pain and seeks the avoidance of pain. Simple? Well, it's a little more complex than that. Most made a spiked collar for difficult, non-retrieving dogs, with the spikes pointing inwards and touching the skin. If the collar was twisted the dog screamed in pain, or rather agony – pain is hardly the word. At the command 'fetch', a dummy or dumb-bell was thrust into

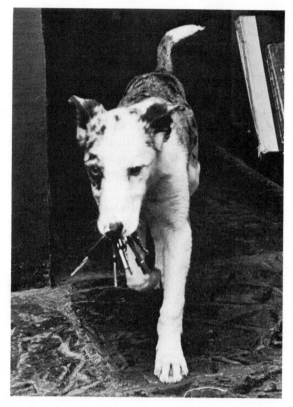

Retrieval of uncongenial object – an essential and often neglected part of lurcher training.

the mouth, and as soon as it touched the gums, the collar was released. Pain – 'fetch' – dummy in mouth – release from pain. 'Fetch' meant release from pain if the task was performed correctly. 'Fetch' must mean something, if not pleasurable, at least not painful. This method required enormous skill, split-second timing and much teaching before the owner could use it on a dog. I know students of Most who vouch for the fact that he had incredible success with even the most savage, unpredictable animals.

Before the reader throws up his hands in horror, exclaiming that he would rather destroy a dog than expose him to such diabolical cruelty, may I remind him that Most took on dogs to train that were about to be destroyed as useless. His methods also laid the foundations for modern forced training methods. May I also add that I doubt if Most ever trained pure-bred sight hounds, who would wilt and snap mentally under such treatment, and remind those fool enough to buy a grown

THE ARTS OF TRAINING AND ENTERING

dog who will not retrieve that they are in for a bad time indeed during any training programme.

Forced retrieving is difficult, make no bones about it. It consists of convincing the dog that it is pleasurable to have a dummy, or object, in its mouth. To start with, have a dog leashed by one's side. With thumb and forefinger behind the canine teeth, prise open the mouth and thrust in the dummy, making a fuss of the dog and uttering the word 'fetch'. Do this several times, and you will become quite dextrous at opening the mouth of the dog with a deft movement of the hands.

Stage two: place the dummy in the dog's mouth and back away from him, uttering the word 'come'. Most dogs will follow you, carrying the dummy with them, usually with bewildered looks on their faces. Praise greatly, alternately offering and removing the dummy to create interest. If your timing is correct, he will associate the dummy in the mouth with the sensation of praise, so he will be more than ready for stage three.

Stage three: this consists of dropping, or rolling, the dummy with the command 'fetch' uttered cajolingly rather like an enticement to a game. If your preliminary training has been completed correctly, he will pick up the dummy and return it. Beware: sight hounds are notoriously difficult to force train.

So on to advanced retrieving, and although to the uninitiated or to the man content to slip a dog at a hare it may all seem like circus tricks, here is the demarcation line between a trainer of dogs and a chap who just runs lurchers. Remember still to make retrieving a game – always a game – and pity the poor beast who has been force trained. For the next stage, drop the dog to the 'stay, lie' position and throw the dummy. He rises to fetch it. 'Stay, lie', drops him again. Allow excitement to build up as he stares at the dummy. Next utter an excited cry of, 'Fetch!' He will race to the dummy and grab it. Crouch and call him, making a fuss of him and praising him greatly when he retrieves it. Repeat a few more times, then quit the game while winning.

As the 'play' progresses, increase the distance between dog and dummy, keeping the dog at the 'lie, stay' position. Again praise on retrieve. Eventually games of hiding the dummy out of sight and sending the puppy to retrieve the object should evolve from such early games, and these will give way to dropping the dummy while walking the dog on a leash and sending the dog back for the dummy. 'Circus tricks,' sneers the smart Alec with dog on slip about to chase a hare. All I can suggest is that the said critic tries to train a circus dog. If he succeeds, then his criticism is accepted. Otherwise it can be dismissed as simply sour grapes.

What is the purpose of such methods? Well, quite simply, imagine

Retrieving training should always be treated as a wild game.

yourself in a position where you are coursing with a friend who merely slips his dog and prays – no training, no retrieving, just chasing; in other words, the task of a coursing greyhound, not a lurcher. Your friend's dog returns, fur in mouth, but with no kill. Dollars to dough-nuts he has made a kill, stood over it awhile and returned without it. Your dog is now in the position of being sent out to retrieve the kill. Gipsies and poachers of old would wait for a shoot to take place, and later in the day would cast their dog over land for game that had been missed. I have always had a passion for retrieving tasks of this nature, and once, when I was twelve, I sent my black mongrel, with scarcely enough greyhound to be termed a lurcher, nearly two miles to fetch a glove. The story is easily checked on; people in my village still talk about this dog.

Advanced retrieving is easily taught and well worth the effort, and it once got my neck out of a legal noose. I was about fourteen, and had snared two rabbits on an estate near Ewenny in Glamorgan. The farm was shot over by a few valley men who jealously guarded the shooting rights, peppering both dogs and people who intruded. I had just passed a line of trees when I saw two men, guns in hand. Fortunately, I saw them before they saw me, dropped my rabbits under a hedge and kicked grass over them. I hopped the fence, and watched their suspicion and resentment as they passed me like two German guards patrolling Treblinka. I sat for an hour, waiting for them to move on, and after that time they did so. 'Fetch', I said, and in a moment I had my two rabbits and was walking for home again. A circus trick? Hardly, merely the work of a dog trainer. Any collie- or retriever-bred lurcher would find the task almost infantile in its simplicity, and it is one a

Dummy hidden: dog about to be sent on.

Sent on to retrieve a dummy.

proficient trainer could teach easily and well a month after basic training and retrieving have been mastered.

The next stage of training is for retrieving a dummy to give way to retrieving a carcass. Now, aspirant lurcher trainer, prepare yourself for a shock. It is a racing certainty that you imagine your dog will be frantic to retrieve the body of a rabbit. It is also a racing certainty that his first encounter with a dead rabbit, or with a dead body of any kind, will alarm him. If he has not seen game killed, then he will be baffled and mystified by the creature you have thrown to him. It is unlikely he will pick it up (unless, of course, you have fed him rabbits or hares). Tease him with the carcass (no, it won't make him hard mouthed – that is a totally different matter), and when he is excited throw him the body to fetch. He will probably fail to retrieve the carcass the first time, but persist and he will. In fact, within an hour he will find the carcass far more alluring than any dummy.

84

I train puppies on squirrels shot by gunners on our local shoot since they make the ideal shape and weight for a first retrieve of a ·'kill'. So repeat the teaching of advanced retrieving with the carcass. The puppy will learn far more quickly now that he has actually retrieved a body, and he can be sent on much further than he would go to fetch an uninteresting dummy.

How then do we approach retrieving over obstacles, fences and so on? Before we come to that we should examine the process of training him to jump.

Reminder: retrieving should be one huge game. Once it palls for the dog, you will have taken a dozen steps back in training.

Jumping

Most greyhound-blooded dogs enjoy jumping, and it is an essential part of training. Although the world high-jump record for dogs is probably still held by an Alsatian, the performances that John Holmes, our best British dog trainer in my opinion, achieved with salukis could easily have challenged and beaten the record, I feel sure. Sight hounds are natural athletes, and Alsatians are neither so lithe or active nor so agile. Holmes could easily have topped the record, as photographs of his salukis jumping enormous obstacles show. Salukis! Who could question that Holmes is our British best?

As to methods of teaching jumping, well, just watch how a hare uses hedges, slips through gaps that would obstruct a terrier. What could be more maddening than to watch a good dog race up and down the hedge, unsuccessfully looking for a gap? What could be more maddening? I'll tell you: a dog that has to be lifted over every fence, every stile, and who howls and barks if left behind, alerting game and possibly gamekeepers, depending on where your morals stand. Unless you are coursing the formidable Salisbury Plains, then a non-jumping dog is a liability and unlikely to come upon a hare on most agricultural land that is full of small fields, hedges and pig wire. No jumping, no hares.

Now listen to the chap who says he owns a dog that finds his way through hedges (which, incidentally, is secret lurcher code for saying, 'I have failed to teach my dog to jump'). In fact, it is one of the most easily taught tasks, even to a grown dog, bought, trained and ruined, as most of the ready-made dogs are.

Basically, there are two main methods of teaching jumping, which are both equally effective, I believe, and both easily taught. Let us begin with the most easily taught method: one that can be used to start six-week-old puppies if one wishes, and which our training fraternity calls 'following on jumping'. Place a bar 4 inches off the floor in a

Advanced jumping: a five-bar gate cleared with ease.

passageway, on the other side of which your puppy is waiting. Call him to you – and as he approaches the obstacle, walk away. He will step over it to you. Praise him – it is nothing by way of a feat, but praise is essential. Next, lift the bar gradually 6 or 7 inches and call him again. If he jumps this, it is a good start. On the next occasion, replace your bar by boards, for he can now crawl under a bar at this height. As he gets older, increase the height of the boards in the passageway. Six feet high is enough for any lurcher and, unless a stunt dog is needed, will suffice for any ordinary hunting country. A five-bar gate is rarely more than 4 feet 6 inches high.

Next comes command jumping, and this is the method used by circus trainers to train dogs to jump through difficult openings, hoops of fire and so forth. It is also the method of training you should adopt if you hope to compete in the games of skill and jumping which are staged at many lurcher shows these days. With dog on leash, and bar 6 inches from the floor, away we go. Up to bar, jump, both you and the dog, with the command, 'Up', and a gentle jerk of the leash. Much praise and patting are needed for such a triumph. Next place the bar at 1 foot:

86

*The result of months of jumping training: an 8 ft 9 in hurdle
cleared with ease.*

same process, same commands, same praise, but more so. One foot is
fine for the first day's progress. Next day, 2 feet, same commands, same
process, same success. Enough for a day. Up and up, until you are
forced to run by the side of the obstacle, jerking his lead to encourage
him to jump. Praise is essential and cannot be overdone. I own a
habitual jumper, an addict for jumping, addicted to leaping and
reward, who will jump back and forth over gates for the slightest degree
of praise. Some dogs love the task, all dogs can be taught it, and without
doubt it gives the owner, or trainer, a great deal of pleasure to watch it
being done.

Konrad Most advocates the command-jumping method while others
settle for the following-on method, where the dog has to jump to get to
its owner. The methods of teaching are different but the action is the
same, and the end-product of both is a dog who is not a damned

87

Retrieved to hand: the author's lurcher retrieves a hare to hand.

liability, howling at fences and stiles and having to be lifted over every obstacle. It is also a dog who can pursue his hare for several fields, not baulking at pig wire and low fences, or trying to scrabble under gates. In fact, it will be a dog well on the way to becoming an all-round lurcher.

This brings us to the completion of basic training. Our dog has taken his passing-out ceremony and passed in style. We now finish this chapter with the most controversial subject of all: entering to quarry. And let us debunk that most common and damnable lie uttered by any lurcherman, 'He coursed and killed the first rabbit he ever saw first time I took him out.' Make a note of such a man, and put a mental marker on him, a huge L, and L for liar not learner – though if he tells such untruths he will probably never be anything but a learner in any case.

Entering to Quarry

Before the advice I am to give – scanty advice at that, I admit, and the reader will see why in a moment – I should like to examine the ways of wild dogs, namely the Cape Hunting dogs (admittedly not a true dog, but they will do), and wolves. A litter is born and fed on the milk of the dam. She eventually weans them on partly digested meat she has regurgitated from her belly. Next, meat is brought to the lair. Then the puppies accompany the parents on a hunt, standing timorously off-scene to watch the kill – a frightening spectacle to wild-dog puppies on the first occasion, so I'm told. After the kill they feed, and every few days they watch yet another kill, eventually joining in. By maybe eighteeen months of age, they have seen many kills, learned many techniques and eventually mastered the art for themselves. In spite of much expert parental tuition, however, the wild-dog puppy will have had many hungry days before he masters the technique.

Now we move on to your puppy, taken from his dam at six or eight weeks old, taught by you, reared by you. Unless you have a trained dog to show him the way and let him benefit from the experience of watching, the way ahead could, and will, be difficult. If he can run with another dog, he can sometimes pick up the skill of catching fairly quickly. If not, it may take some time – a very long time occasionally. But it will come, of that be sure – so tear up the advertisement you had prepared, 'Dog ready for starting', and persevere. Moreover, unless you, the trainer, are capable of running alongside a rabbit and snap-ping it up with your mouth, the dog trained without copying a trained coursing dog will miss many, many rabbits before he makes a kill. And if you can do this party piece, why in hell do you think you need a dog? It is an agent you need, for you will be a sensation in any circus. Stupid comment? Well, let's see, as we come to some commonly given advice on training.

Here are some samples to start with. Tegner, in his erudite book, *Wild Hares*, mentions a friend who had a whippet that would course hares, but would tumble and play with them. After asking how she was turned into an efficient hare killer, Tegner was told that his friend had tied a live rat to the dog's leg. I had thought that such imbecilic comments were confined to my own areas of experience, and I am delighted to find out it is nationwide and not just restricted to the Midlands and South Wales.

Our favourite make-or-break tale, and it is usually break, I assure you, concerns putting a live rabbit in a shed with a young lurcher and leaving it there until the dog has killed the rabbit, even starving the dog into murdering the terrified bunny. Drabble mentions this in his *Pedigree Unknown*, and he, too, states that it does not work. The banging and bumping of the terrified rabbit hurling itself around the shed will usually be sufficient to put any dog off rabbits and to frighten the wits out of a sensible puppy. While we are on the subject, giving a greyhound a live rat before a race is supposed to stop a track dog from fighting. It doesn't, and it's a bit rough on the rat as well.

On the other hand, Harry Lees of Burton, a good lurcherman and one whose skill at choosing a promising puppy out of a litter puts me to shame, believes that a dead rabbit on a lure, jerked hither and thither by one of those bicycle-wheel contraptions used at terrier races, helps a dog to pick up his quarry. It may do, and Harry is certainly an expert at early entering.

It is surprising how many puppies who see a live rabbit, or a dead one on a lure, will try to pin it with their feet. Sometimes a terrier tries this with a rat, and once is usual, but no more. A lurcher, however, may be eighteen months before he learns to kill properly, unless he can copy a grown dog that is killing well. In those intervening months, however, he will have learned a great deal, and each mistake he makes is positively helpful in the furtherance of his training. Well, I did warn you that the way ahead would be hard, and to illustrate it further let me describe a typical session of hunts that precede a kill.

It is morning, and the dew is heavy on the ground, the time of day when rabbits, still fooled by the safety of the night, are feeding far from the sanctuary of their burrows. The dew is still silvery, showing lines or striations of dryness that indicate a rabbit's belly has dried a line of grass as the animal has raced back and forth to its lair – a habit of rabbits anxious to remain alive in a world hostile to their kind. Your puppy of eight months has lost its awkward puppy movements and is rapidly becoming a thing of beauty. He sniffs each dry furrow anxiously, eager for the prey whose body scent is still strong within the furrows – an exciting scent that brings back race memories of his sight-hound ancestry. A rabbit near to the hedge, a mere yard or so from cover, lifts its ears and shows its scut, and the puppy runs at it excitedly – a fool's game, with the sanctuary of the burrow a mere yard away. We find our dog gazing down the burrow, mystified as to the speed of the rabbit.

Later, if he is bred properly and has brains enough to justify the title of lurcher rather than coursing greyhound, he will ignore such prey, gauging, assessing, calculating his chances of taking his quarry and rejecting the idea of a run at rabbits sitting close to home, but today, today he is a puppy, and in puppies, as in youth, hope springs eternal. So every rabbit is fair game, every rabbit potential prey. Four or five runs follow, all equally unsuccessful, all equally energy sapping, all equally frustrating to the owner. The morning drags on and the dew

90

*Overshooting the quarry: a common fault in puppies unused to
the ways of rabbits.*

dries: a time when only fools are feeding, and then we see him – a fool, a
genuine fool, an adult buck a full fifty yards from cover. Pray there is no
burrow in that long grass to the left. Leash on puppy now, no need to
frighten the rabbit, stalk it, stalk it like a cat. Closer now, closer, and
still the damned dog hasn't noticed it, but neither has the rabbit
become aware of you. A triangle, 50 yards along the sides, 50 yards
between you and the rabbit, the rabbit and its lair. Closer if you can,
quietly, your heart almost missing a beat. The gentle straining on the
leash bespeaks the fact the dog has seen the quarry, but ears are up on
both rabbit and dog, both aware now of each other's presence. At a
sharp movement from the prey – slip the dog. He eats up the distance,
easily overtaking its prey, and then he is on it. He is totally unable to
miss, and bends down his neck, that neck like a drake, to snap up the
prey. Easy, all too easy . . . and then the sudden realization comes to
you as to how the rabbit, hunted by all, remains still common. At the

91

moment of impact the rabbit turns on its own length, leaving the dog careering on for ten yards. Again he turns, but as he eats up the distance the rabbit suddenly jinks and we find the dog gazing down a hole for a scut that has vanished from sight.

Rabbits are not easy meat, they rarely feed far from their burrows and are for ever alert. Such runs will be very common before a dog makes a kill, and the hunter will be sorely tempted to contemplate a 'Lurcher dog just starting' advertisement in *Exchange and Mart*. Persist, however, and sooner or later your dog will make a kill. One of the best coursing whippets I have ever seen – one capable of taking hare, a rare feat in spite of what coursing books tell you – was over a year old before she took her first rabbit. It is often a skill that is slowly learned unless, as I say, it can be copied from a dog that is already killing.

One constantly hears such comments as, 'I sold him because he wouldn't pick up' (which means 'catch a rabbit' in lurcher parlance). 'How can I get him to pick up?' is another question that the desperate often ask, though the pseudo-expert would have sold the dog at the first failure. Frankly, while there is something to be said for the use of the lure, Harry Lee's speciality, there is no substitute for experience of the real kind – experience on live quarry, failure at live quarry, and ultimately success. Advice to men who have a dog that will not pick up: run him regularly. Still won't pick up? Then run him some more. Some animals are slower to learn than others, yet eventually make excellent hunting dogs.

David James, who specializes in collie/greyhound hybrids, says that the best often run rabbit many times before making a kill, content to run and herd them rather than snatch one up. Bowling a rabbit, keeping it down with their feet, is another common early training fault with this priceless cross. Don't give up and sell him – persist, and then persist some more. I rank every failure I get with a dog as a fault of mine, not of the dog's, and I am reluctant to write off such an animal as worthless. There are few dogs with sight-hound blood who are complete failures at some form of coursing, be it in rabbiting or at the staple quarry, the hare. I know several people in my locality who are forever buying and selling dogs, labelling untrained dogs as useless and passing them on. This is a tragedy, but what is an even greater tragedy is that such people are labelled typical lurchermen. Sadly, they are reasonably representative of our present-day lurcher keepers. I shall refrain from using the word trainer on such people, it would be a misnomer – meddlers, ruiners, spoilers they may be, but hardly trainers.

Unfortunately, most lurcher dealers fall into this category, trading in failure dogs, passing them on from person to person, acting as a canine stock exchange in the forlorn hope that the dogs will land in the hands of someone who can train them satisfactorily. Still more sadly, few of these dogs do end up in the care of someone with the correct skills, and the greyhound blood leads them to accept their unhappy fates with the minimum of trauma, at least of outward trauma. People who sell a dog as a failure without giving it a chance deserve a big A, not as a mark of excellence, merely as the hallmark of the amateur. Again, I repeat, there are few dogs that, given the right treatment, will not make useful hunting dogs. There are few useless lurchers, but a great many useless trainers. Write off a dog during training and you are actually acknowledging not the dog's but your own failure.

If any dog is given enough practice, it will learn to pick up quarry quite well – perhaps not hare, since that does require a rather super-athletic dog, but rabbiting dogs can be made out of any reasonably shaped lurcher with sight-hound blood. If one is in any doubt as to this statement, I can assure the reader that I know two farmers who had dogs given them as absolute failures, only to allow them complete freedom to roam, make mistakes, make bad runs, and ultimately become first-class coursing lurchers – though a little wild for my liking, I must admit, as I have a fetish about obedience, and complete freedom

A near miss – dog turns hare but fails to pick it up.

93

Picking up – a skill that often takes some while to learn.

is not conducive to total obedience. Pattinson states that he takes his dogs when he goes out around his farm, and that they learn a great deal through their encounters and courses at ground game. Of course, the problem with allowing any lurcher complete freedom is that they will soon kill all ground game, take to poaching neighbouring land and, once they have exhausted all sources of game, are likely to turn their attention to sheep.

With basic training now complete, your dog is probably hunting up rabbits, sitting, lying, staying on command, taking game – at least rabbits by day – and retrieving. It is time to further his and your training by another couple of stages and to tackle the skills of working with lamps and nets.

94

9 *Lamping and Net Work*

Lamping

Lamping is the art, or science, call it which you will, of taking ground game with artificial lights and dogs. In pre-war times, it was common practice to drive an estate car or pick-up truck around the fields with lights ablaze and to shoot the feeding rabbits, mesmerized by the unfamiliar sound of the motor and the blaze of headlamps. Walsh mentions that he has slipped dogs from such a motor vehicle and caught rabbits in that way.

Today, however, the lamper adopts far more sophisticated devices to take rabbits and hares and even deer. These are improvements on hunting from a motor vehicle. So sophisticated are they that poachers, and frankly most lampers are poachers, are currently causing great concern among the keepered estates of the country. Punishment for lampers involves not only a stiff fine under the Night Poaching Act, but also the confiscation of lamp, battery and other equipment. Many poachers appeal to magistrates for the return of their apparatus, but I personally know of no court that has sanctioned such an appeal.

First for the equipment. Walsh, in his *Lurchers and Long Dogs*, shows a photograph of a man with lamping equipment using a huge battery slung inside an even bigger haversack. I can only think that Colonel Walsh never lamped, or else that the photograph must have been taken many years ago before small 12-volt batteries were invented. The man in the photograph looks more equipped for an army field punishment than a night's lamping. Carrying a car battery would exhaust the strongest man in a matter of a mile, and many lampers hunt all night. The most commonly used battery is the small Lucas 12-volt motorbike battery, although I believe there is an even smaller, neater type of battery produced in Japan. This battery is now connected up to a spotlight – the quartz halide types are most commonly used – and the device fitted with a switch which can flick the beam on or off at a moment's notice.

Having described the basic equipment, we come to the finer points. Poachers, and, as I have said, most lampers are poachers, do not want a powerful beam illuminating the countryside, alerting rabbits and

Lamping – dog on slip.

A lamping kit – comprising a 'blacked in' beam, a shielded beam and a
12 volt motor bike battery encased in a leather carrier.

police alike. Therefore the beam is 'painted in', the perimeter of the
glass spotlight being painted black, usually with a matt black bitumastic type of paint, leaving only a tiny gap through which the light can
shine. This tiny but powerful beam is now practically undetectable to
any gamekeeper, whereas the open beam could probably be seen for
miles. Another method of curbing the beam is to fit the spotlight with a
cowl, usually made by cutting the bottom out of a large tin and
attaching it to the lamp with tape. The shining tin plate must, of course,
be treated with the same black bitumastic paint.

It is also possible to buy lamping devices, though these are a little
cumbersome for poaching and are not as mobile as a spotlight attached
to battery equipment. Swinford night lamps are enormously powerful
lamps, and although, I am told, they were originally designed for
keepers and security men, they are frequently used by poachers. They
are box-shaped and frankly a little clumsy, but fitting them with a pistol
grip makes them more easy to use. Such lamps are fitted with their own
battery chargers and need only to be plugged into the mains to recharge
the lamp. Lucas batteries, of course, need constant attention, topping
up and so on, and have to be fitted to a battery charger to recharge the

battery. One tip about carrying a wet battery in a haversack: sooner or later, leaping a ditch or running with the lamp will cause some of the sulphuric acid to spill from the battery and corrode the haversack, leaving huge holes and not only ruining the carrying bag, but allowing acid to eat holes in one's clothes and so forth. This can be remedied by obtaining an empty plastic detergent bottle – the gallon variety – trimming the top and placing the battery inside. Care of the battery and daily checking is very necessary as the batteries are expensive. At the time of writing, they cost between £16 and £17, but properly cared for, topped up and kept recharged, they will last the hunter for a very long time.

To put it quite simply, lamping consists of climbing quietly over the gate of a field, keeping the dog under control – preferably on a slip – and shining the beam around the field. At first the impact such a scene makes on the hunter is quite startling, for whereas rabbit shapes are seldom seen, the ruby eyes of the rabbit catching the beam shine like coals in the darkness. To the uninitiated, hunting in this manner must

Lamping: fox caught in beam.

appear absolute slaughter, for they believe the rabbits must be mesmerized by the beam and thus fall easy victims for the dog. This is sometimes so, and I have kept rabbits in a squat for so long using a lamp that I have caught them by walking up to them (still shining the lamp) and simply picking up the frightened animal. This squatting is not through terror, however, but is usually in the hope that absence of movement will allow the hunter to miss the rabbit, and this would be so if it were not for the ruby eyes. Squatting rabbits who refuse to move also evade some lurchers since some dogs usually run only moving quarry. A skilled dog, however, soon learns to pick up squatters and will make a rapid and easy haul for the hunter.

Most rabbits simply hightail it for home when lamped, on the other hand, and when an area has been lamped with any degree of regularity, they will race for home as soon as they see the beam. This is called educating to the lamp. In other words, the rabbit has realized that the lamp is the first sign that danger is about to threaten. Skilled lampers – poachers who live by lamping – will rarely hunt the same ground regularly, favouring instead a run every few weeks or so, so as not to educate the rabbits to the significance of the beam.

What would be a description of the ideal lamping night? Lamping in bright moonlight is frankly madness, for although the rabbits are usually feeding far from their burrows, they watch your approach with more interest than fear and then run for home before you get within range – that is, close enough to slip a dog. The ideal night, a lamper's dream, is pitch black (most lampers keep a calendar of the moon phases and decline to hunt during the full moon) and, if possible, very windy. The wind muffles the sound of the approaching hunter and so avoids alerting the rabbit before the sport begins. Some lampers even favour a slight drizzle, though for the life of me I cannot think why. A still night with no wind will usually result in a small haul, and no catches at all if the land has been lamped regularly. Biologists tell us that rabbits are unintelligent beasts, and the biologists are probably right. The rabbit, however, has a highly developed sense of danger to compensate for his lack of brain, and soon runs for home at the slightest sign of trouble.

Hares may also be lamped, and if they can be kept in the beam long enough an indifferent lurcher will take them – a lurcher which would have had no chance of catching a hare by coursing by day will often take hares fairly readily in the lamp. Hares panic badly when lamped for the first time, though they soon educate to the beam, and do so far more quickly than rabbit, in fact. Such is the panic of a hare lamped for the first time that, to evade a dog, it will actually run back towards the man holding the lamp. One of the first hares I caught with a lamp was killed by running into my foot, which I placed out to trip it up as it

99

approached – unsporting perhaps, but lamping is quite serious business to many and not really sport at all. I know many hunters who do not work, but live by selling their lamped rabbits caught during the moonless nights of the month. Such hunters/poachers will rarely allow a lamp dog to run a hare, for not only does a hare put up quite a run, so leaving the dog exhausted and not fit for another course for some time, but at the time of writing each rabbit caught will fetch £1 whereas hare meat is not very popular and therefore difficult to sell. The effort expended to take one hare would enable the dog to kill several very saleable rabbits instead.

What of the dogs, and the most suitable breeds for lamping? Here you have a choice indeed from all the breeds mentioned, plus the myriad crosses advertised as deerhound/greyhound which are none the worse for dubious ancestry. Frankly, I like collie/greyhound types for all work, for not only do they learn lamping quickly, but a thousand generations of dogs expected to run a hundred miles a day makes a good base on which to produce a lamping dog. Lamp dogs can, and do, run twenty miles a night – short, sharp runs admittedly, but distance is distance any way you look at it. Furthermore, the collie is a sagacious beast, and lurchers bred from them learn the knack of lamping and its million little skills far more quickly than other breeds. Coupled with this is the fact that they are easily taught to retrieve – a skill essential to all lamping dogs unless one wants to run twenty miles a night and pick up the game on which your dog is standing. This failure to retrieve game is a fault among many dogs with sight-hound ancestry, as I have mentioned.

Another quality, and I use the word quality rather than fault, is 'hunting up' – in other words, running game by scent instead of the dog watching the movement of the rabbit in the beam. This is also a great nuisance if the dog loses its rabbit in the hedgerow and prompty begins to hunt it up by scent, thereby putting to ground every other rabbit within 200 yards. This is why a great many lurchermen maintain there can be no all-round lurchers, for a dog required to hunt up as well as course a hare will almost certainly put its nose down when it loses a rabbit. This can be overcome by (a) running the dog from a slip, either a professionally made slip like the Altcar slip, or a Heath Robinson device made from binder twine (free and no problem if lost) such as I use; and (b) absolute and immediate obedience, returning instantly to the owner as soon as the rabbit is caught or lost. I must stress that this obedience has to be of a very high standard if the dog is to be called off hunting by nose, for dogs that hunt by nose are frequently reluctant to obey return commands. 'Deafing you out' is what it is called in the Midlands. It is difficult to get a dog to leave a red-hot scent, particularly when the return command is a hissed whistle so as not to alert the other rabbits that mischief is afoot. Thus, early obedience training has to be done, and done thoroughly. The dog must consider it its duty to return the moment it loses the rabbit. Such obedience is certainly possible, and although it may prove a mammoth task with a saluki (far too hard for me to attempt, I confess), dogs with traces of pastoral blood in their veins are usually amenable to discipline of this kind, though it is never easy to teach a dog to this high standard.

Again, many people do not teach a lamping dog to jump, and in fact many discourage jumping in their lurchers. The logic is fairly obvious. Dancing in the dark is one thing, jumping quite another, and while a human being would be most reluctant to jump into total blackness with no knowledge of the perils and pitfalls on the other side of the fence, lurchers, particularly those hot on the scent of game, will not ask why and wherefore before leaping a hedge while oblivious to the dangers on the other side. I'm not all that happy about this logic, however, for I know many lamping dogs who are superb jumpers, and the one featured contemplating the high jump in the plate (page 0-00), is a great athlete and a very good lamper. For the sake of caution, I might add that I have seen lamp dogs terribly crippled by leaping into the unknown, as well as quite a few dead ones. I suppose the logical approach to this topic is to examine (or get to know) the land one is to hunt by daylight, which isn't always practicable for poachers!

Size is another matter for controversy among the lamping fraternity. Most Midland lampers tend to favour a smaller dog, measuring 20 to 22 inches at the shoulder, for such dogs are agile, nimble and quick on the turn. Further north, particularly around Liverpool, the larger dog finds favour, some say because the fields there are larger than those in the Midlands. George Smith, who wrote the chapter on lamping in *Lurchers and Long Dogs*, says that a considerably larger dog is often useful – he mentions one of 30 inches that he states was a world beater. Size is actually unimportant in comparison with agility – the nimble dog is always superior to the fast dog at lamping. The incredible Dai Fish actually lamped a lightly built collie with considerable success, but it was, in its day, a very agile dog, not as fast as a lurcher, so Dai had to choose his rabbits, running his dog at easy kills. Some amazing mongrel dogs with greyhound blood do often make moderate, if not very fast, lamp dogs. Pattinson describes his ideal all-round lurcher as a 22- to 24-inch dog, and though I might extend the top and bottom limits by an inch, I believe he comes close to the mark. Between 23 and 25 inches is perhaps a good all-round size for daytime coursing, and also for work at night.

We have dealt with the lamp, the breed of dog and size of dog, so what of the training? This can be very hard or ridiculously easy, depending on whether or not one has a trained dog to hand at the time. A six-month-old puppy which is allowed to watch a rabbit being chased by a grown dog soon learns to pick up the skill, particularly if it is a dog bred from the bitch lamping the rabbit. Mothers teach their progeny rather more easily than they teach other dogs, so a great number of countrymen say, and there is perhaps some truth in it. If one lacks a trained dog, then it can be very hard to teach a lamping dog the skills, particularly in districts that are over-lamped and where rabbits are so educated to the beam that the first flicker of a light puts them back. Five years ago I scorned the use of an old dog in teaching a puppy, a bitch called Bear, and resolved to try training from scratch. It proved quite hard, and it was three months before Bear learned the skill. I hasten to add she was saluki bred, and not the easiest to train – game but stupid summed up Bear, I'm afraid. Still, do not despair. Persist, and if you try and fail, try, try and try again. Please forget about purchasing from the 'trained for lamping' advertisement that keeps springing to your mind when your dog has failed a dozen times. Sooner or later the penny will drop.

The best place to start a dog is in a part of the country where the rabbits are unfamiliar with the lamp – a difficult place to find since the lurcher began to vie with the Jack Russell as the most popular breed. Choose both night and spot with care, for early success makes a dog, and a succession of failures produces a dispirited animal and a frustrated owner. The field gate is open now, the dog on slip. On into the field, weighing up wind and weather and the proximity of any hedge to the feeding place of the rabbits. On with the beam, and the first few hightail it back to the hedge, another sits alert a foot away from its warren. Pass him by – he will be home the moment the dog moves. Another, another, another . . . all out of reach, all feeding close. Don't despair, you have all night, and all night is what it may take. Wait for your rabbit, one that will squat until you are nearly on top of it, fixed, as it were, by the beam. As soon as you are up to it, be prepared to slip your dog. With luck you may get so close to the rabbit that you have to touch it to make it move. Forget about hunt law, meaning a fair chance for the prey. The lamper isn't out for fair coursing, he is out to make a catch. Slip the dog as close to the rabbit as possible, as soon as it moves and the dog shows an interest in the movement. With luck, and a hell of a lot of luck, I must admit, the dog will take the rabbit. It is far more likely that he will miss several before he succeeds in making a kill.

Lamping remains, despite the chances, the most effective form of coursing rabbits with a dog, and enormous hauls can be made by well-trained dogs and a skilled man. Skill is needed, however, on both sides of the team, as is coordination between dog and man, each knowing his allotted task and each aware of the other's part in the hunt. It is truly a pleasure to watch a skilled lamper work with a dog he has reared and trained from a puppy. Lamping is increasing, particularly illegal lamping, and the rabbit population, already thinned by myxomatosis, takes quite a beating in some areas as a consequence. Near one town in the Midlands, noted for its rather unsavoury lurcher owners, it is a joke among the police that, as soon as a rabbit gets up in a field, five men with dogs and beams leap from behind a tree to take it.

Lamping is basically a one dog v. one rabbit exercise, not for sporting reasons, since lamping is quite big business in some parts of the country, but because of the dangers involved in running two dogs over fields littered with hazards at dead of night. Collision is fairly inevitable, and as lurchers can frequently clock up 30 miles an hour or so on a run, the effect of an impact can be pretty frightening and often fatal. It is also true that few dogs give of their best when there is a danger of colliding with another dog in the darkness. Furthermore, lamping is pot-hunting or hunting for profit these days, when rabbits will fetch £1 apiece, and two dogs grabbing and tugging at a rabbit do little to improve its saleable value. Hence it is good logic to run only one dog at one rabbit when lamping.

There is also the problem of retrieving standards deteriorating when two dogs are run together, or even hunted together, for that matter. The element of jealousy is strong in all dogs, particularly in sight hounds, and many will simply race off and hide a rabbit when a pair are run at a quarry. Many lurchers will similarly refuse to return the rabbit to the owner if he has another dog on a slip at his side. This jealousy will usually manifest itself in running around a field with the rabbit in the mouth, just out of the trainer's reach, which is not only annoying, but also alerting every other rabbit in the field. Sometimes two lurchers will work well together, but they lack the cohesive togetherness of a one man and his dog team.

As I have said, lamping is fairly big business, and although the penalty for poaching rabbits at night (the Night Poaching Act) are fairly steep, it does not usually deter the lamper, who can usually pay his fine out of a night's lamping. Furthermore, lamping was not until recently regarded as a particularly serious offence, being frankly treated as a joke, a minor peccadillo, by most magistrates. Things are changing, however, for as shoots grow more expensive and less easy to come by, so even the humble bunny comes to be protected by the owner of these shoots. The lamping of deer, and even sheep, has moreover been given a great deal of publicity in the press, and very bad publicity at that, and magistrates have begun to fine lampers quite heavily. One team of lampers, recently convicted of taking deer, was fined a total of £2,000, and with the laws designed to prevent poaching becoming stiffer year by year, the convicted rabbit poacher is going to come in for a rough time in the near future.

Yet lamping is still on the increase, in spite of the potential risks involved. Why, the reader may ask? Quite simply, the risks are not particularly high provided one sticks to rabbit and gives deer parks a clear miss, even when in pursuit of coneys. Deer parks are virtual death-traps to the humble lamper of rabbits with a whippet type of lurcher totally incapable of taking deer. Even though I went into the subject thoroughly in *Rogues and Running Dogs*, we should review the reasons here for why lamping is not particularly risky, or to put it another way, was not particularly risky until the recent spate of bad publicity. First, rabbits usually live on the pastures of farmland and are not rated highly as game by most shoots, technically because they are not really game at all, so the farmer is not usually too worried if one or two coneys are removed from his land. Next, in spite of the townies' opinions of country people, a farmer's life is a hard one, and bearing in mind that most lamping is done on gusty, windy, black inclement nights, most farmers are reluctant to leave their warm beds just to pursue a wraith-like figure after a few rabbits. Even if his land is rented as a shoot, it is the shoot's not the farmer's duty to prevent poachers, so he is likely to leave the poacher to his own devices and turn over in bed and sleep rather than venture out to protect rabbits that are no longer his direct concern. I know many lampers who work right up to a farmyard, secure in the knowledge that the farmer is totally indifferent to poachers of rabbits.

Even so, assume that a farmer does leave his house to investigate a beam shining across his land. The lamper is probably used to the darkness of the night and, like the Arabs, steals silently away. If pursuit is attempted, a quick flash with the beam will leave the farmer temporarily blinded by the light, and this makes escape easier still. Policemen are also somewhat reluctant to leave warm Panda cars to cross muddy fields in pursuit of a rabbit-hunting poacher, particularly when one considers that many lampers work in gangs, and I, for one, would not like to be a bobby set about by some of the rogues I know. Thus, provided the game is left in peace, the lamper is, or used to be, fairly safe.

But kill a pheasant or two, and that is an entirely different matter. Even knocking the odd nesting cock bird out of a tree with a catapult is tantamount to a declaration of war to most landowners. There is something oddly protective in most farmers' attitudes towards pheasant, even if they are birds which have just escaped the massacre from a near-by shoot. If he loses a pheasant or two, or worse still, finds any gone from stock which he has put down, the first sign of a lamp on his land will usually see him reaching for the phone and dialling 999.

A dog unsafe with stock, however, will certainly be the downfall of a lamping man. A light flashing around the fields is unlikely on its own to upset a farmer, but baleful bleating from his sheep will bring him down on any intruder in double-quick time. Any lamping poacher worth his salt has his dogs rock-steady with sheep and such-like before venturing out after a rabbit. Furthermore, a dog that barks, or opens up, as they say in lurcher circles, is a hazard, since it will seem to set the whole countryside alive. This is why most advertisements for lamping dogs read 'strong, silent and fast' as the appraisal of the dog they are trying to sell. Whippets, Pharaoh hounds and Ibizans are notoriously noisy, and are not really suitable for the night-time poacher.

My favourite story about lamping was told me by a friend who is on the correct side of the law: a retired bobby who also helps with part-time keeping on quite a large estate. Rabbit poachers there were overlooked, or treated as only a bit of a nuisance, until one fool of a poacher started to catch partridges and pheasants. Now any reasonably capable keeper will know whether or not the stock of birds on his land is shrinking, and the sight of feathers littering a field will confirm his suspicions. At first my friend contacted a security firm, and bought a police-trained Alsatian, but found that this city-trained dog barked at sheep and cattle as well as intruders and was giving him sleepless nights. At first he was upset about his failure to control the poachers, particularly as he was living rent-free in a cottage on the estate – a cottage given to him through his reputation for being a diligent officer of the law. One night he happened to find a bull out on the road near his house, and forthwith went round in his car to report the matter to the owner of the bull – a farmer who lived about a mile away. As he drove up the farmer's drive all hell was let loose – a screaming, gobbling, sound, like a cross between the noises made by a turkey and an electric saw was how he described it. The farmer kept guinea-fowl, and these are far more alert to intruders than any dog. They are also highly paranoid and noisy, so, fired with the idea, he bought a dozen or more chicks and allowed them the liberty of a shoot. It would today be one hell of a challenge to poach that estate, for, unlike his dog, guinea-fowl accept sheep and cattle as part of the scenery, but a lamp and a dog will set them screaming fit to wake the dead.

Not even police hell-bent on taking poachers will go to the lengths to tramp across fields to pursue them. They simply transmit their whereabouts to the station and then ride around the lanes watching for a deserted car parked inconspicuously in some gateway. All they have to do then is wait for the poacher to return and be caught red-handed with the game he has taken. This is where most poachers get taken, and large numbers of gamekeepers, now wise to the ways of lampers, will disconnect the leads on the car or let the tyres down before awaiting their return. Well over 80 per cent of the prosecuted poachers whom I know were apprehended at their car. The experienced poacher usually leaves his car a mile or so away from his lamping spot to avoid detection. Funnily enough, even as I write this, I hear that a poacher has counter-petitioned a gamekeeper who let down the poacher's car tyres and damaged his distributor. The result of the case will be most interesting, I am sure.

Cars out in the early morning are frequently turned over, or searched, by the police. This is an occupational hazard for a lamper, but provided he has a place near by where he has written permission to take rabbits, he is in the clear. No policeman in his right mind would venture an opinion as to where certain rabbits were taken – he will to the poacher, perhaps, but hardly in a court of law. He will undoubtedly check that the poacher does indeed have permission on the land where he has supposedly obtained his rabbits, then shrug his shoulders and put the whole matter down to experience.

Badgers can sometimes be a problem if one's dogs are not broken to them, and the best way to break them to badger is quite simply not to encourage them to attack them. One often sees advertisements for lurchers who can draw badger as well as perform their customary tasks of coursing. Such a dog will be useless for lamping. Badgers are nocturnal, and it is almost certain that the lamping man will meet one sooner or later. They are creatures best left alone, and well alone at that, for not only are they loosely protected by the law, but they are of little economic value (their flesh is inedible and their fur useless). They are also invulnerable to a dog's bite and are mighty fighters.

Many boast of having dogs that will kill a badger, but I have yet to see a dog do so. Even the bravest dog will be bested by this shuffling, ponderous, ursine shape – a member of the stoat family, in spite of his appearance. It is best never to encourage any dog to chase one should it amble into the beam, for the ensuing fight will do much to damage the dog, rendering it crippled and maimed. It should be remembered by those men who tell tales of badger-killing lurchers that Brock was used to test the courage of pit bull terriers and Blue Pauls – fighting dogs designed for combat, and not lightly built lurchers bred for coursing. Few dogs will attack a badger unless encouraged to do so, and it is bad policy to try one's lamping dogs against them. A lamping dog is a meat provider which will give you ten times its value in rabbits. To run one against a ponderous brawler whose economic value is nothing is absolute madness.

With the right training and perseverance, the lamping lurcher is really a provider, the pot-hunter supreme, the poacher's dog *par excellence*. I know many who practically live by the proceeds of lamping, but a final word of caution for the lamping poacher of rabbits. A wind of change is rustling the pages of the game laws, and poaching by night will soon no longer be the joke it has been – a joke where even magistrates consider the night poacher to be a bit of a giggle. There is, at the moment of writing, a pressure group earnestly and efficiently pushing through a new set of laws that will make night poaching quite a serious offence, and once such laws have been passed, as seems inevitable, stinging punishments for offenders will be on the cards. The 1831 Game Laws have, since the Second World War, been treated in a casual manner by police, magistrates and poachers alike. The next ten years will see a vast change in this attitude, I'm afraid.

Net Work

This is the most difficult task to teach a lurcher, and few dogs that can work gate net and long nets are ever sold. It requires months of work and a great deal of expert training to attempt to train a dog to the high standards required for net work. Frankly, unless a dog has collie or retriever blood, it is very difficult to teach him to work with nets. Few sight-hound matings, such as deerhound/greyhound, saluki/greyhound, are tractable enough to train to this task.

First things first: the dog has to be absolutely under control, dropping to command and coming on to command. Unless a dog is superbly trained it is useless, and also costly, to teach him to long net. Furthermore, a dog must be rock-steady to livestock, and so it is unwise to start training a dog to net work until he is perhaps eighteen months of age. It should be pointed out, however, that such a dog, once trained, can help the hunter to take an incredibly large haul of game in the night.

Long Netting

Long netting is highly profitable if the game abounds, and in the pre-myxomatosis days hauls of over a hundred rabbits a night were common. In some districts it may still be profitable to long net, but to set a long net needs practice and skill. There will usually be very few head of quarry taken during first tries with long netting, unless, of course, one has an experienced helper. Quite simply, long netting and

A long net.

lurcher work is done at night and consists of spreading a long net between the rabbits and their warren. The day prior to the netting, the hunter should acquaint himself with the lie of the land and remove any obstructions that may snag a net as he unfurls it, keeping it tight at the top, slack at the base. The long netter must unfurl his nets rapidly, staking every few yards and taking every measure to be as quiet as possible.

After the netting is completed, a dog is put in at the other end of the field and allowed to hunt up the rabbits, which promptly and quickly run for home, only to become entangled in the net. Speed is not important, and elderly lurchers are often best at this game. Nose is

important, however, for unlike the lamping lurcher, the long-net
lurcher needs to hunt head down. Night-hunting poachers of old
preferred a dog who was reluctant to pick up, as not only did the dog not
then crash into the nets, sending the *tout ensemble* flying, but most
rabbits reached the nets undamaged to be necked by the man behind
the nets. Obviously, long-net work requires more than one man to aid
in the job, and it was more often a quartet, three men and a dog, that
was the most satisfactory grouping for long netting. The problem of
working the long net with a dog arises, of course, in the event of the dog
diving into the net to catch the rabbit. Thus, a very steady dog is
priceless, and after a few bad goes, the dog soon learns that rabbits in
the nets are forbidden but that one which turns back is fair game. Few
people train dogs to such a state of perfection today, which is a pity, for
we are letting the pot-hunting lurcher degenerate into a dog that is a
sight hunter pure and simple.

Gate Netting

This is a dying art, and few dogs today can work a gate net properly.
Gate nets are used where hares, and sometimes rabbits, use a gate or
gateway as an entry and exit to the feeding ground. This can easily be

Gate netting.

detected when the runs under a gate are examined. Perhaps the surest way of determining whether a gate is being used as an escape route is to go early in the morning, disturb the still feeding hares and rabbits and note which way they run. The old-time poachers were high in bush-craft, and it is a skill, like gate netting, that is now quite rare.

Once the gate was found and the run under the gate noted, the old-fashioned gate nets so beloved by poachers of tradition, though not used today, were set by balancing fairly large stones on the portion of net that covered the top of the gate and fairly small stones on area at the ground level, making quite sure that the run was covered completely. The task completed, the dog was encouraged to jump the gate and work the field, always towards the net. If the dog was diligent and hunted well, he turned the hare back towards the gate. Speed was not essential, but good nose was and is. Most good net dogs are really in their dotage anyway, so the hare, contemptuous of the pestering of this dog, would lope back to the gate, hit the net and bring down the whole tangle on top of him. Modern gate nets, however, are simply miniature long nets stretched across the gateway (with the gate opened), which thus trap the hare as it darts through the gap between the gateposts. Gate netting in the hands of the skilful is an extremely efficient way of taking game. The dog must be taught that he must not attack the tangle of netting and hares, and be absolutely obedient to every command. Gate netting is a skilled job, a far cry from the man who is content to slip a lurcher at a feeding hare. A point to note, however, is that no gate netter should work without a torch, for foxes often use the runs frequented by hares, and untangling a fox at night without a lamp is a hair-raising task.

Gusty nights are, of course, fairly essential for the venture, as not only will the sound of the wind muffle the sound of the nets man at work, but the wind also reduces the strength of human scent around the gates and warrens – scent which is, on a still night, enough to get the quarry to turn back and avoid becoming tangled in the nets.

10 *The Quarry Itself*

The Rabbit

Unlike the hare, which, along with the badger, must, as Geoffrey Sparrow says, rank as one of the oldest inhabitants of Britain, the rabbit is probably not a native of these islands. Speculation as to how he came here is wide: Phoenicians, Romans, Normans, all seem to be contestants for the 'who introduced the rabbit' stakes. Certainly the Romans knew the rabbit, and the natives of the Balearic Islands once sent a frantic request to the Emperor Augustus, begging the use of soldiers to ferret the islands and reduce the number of rabbits, which had grown to plague proportions. Pliny the Elder, who was a highly esteemed naturalist (though none too wise, as he died from sulphur dioxide poisoning when his scientific zeal took him too close to the eruption of Vesuvius that destroyed Pompeii), tells this tale. I doubt if Augustus was concerned as much with rabbits at this time as he was with 'eagles', having lost several legions in battle against the Germans that same year. Harting speculates that the Romans brought the rabbit, but as with most nineteenth-century sporting writers, his work is simply educated guesswork.

Sufficient to say, however, that William the Conqueror brought a warrener among his troops, either to hunt rabbits in England, or maybe to set up enclosed warrens. There are twelfth-century midden piles which reveal bones of rabbits among their contents, and at that we will leave the rest to speculation. The coney arrived, and he spread, and spread, and spread . . . enough to alter the face of England and modify both its flora and fauna. After the rat, it may be argued that the rabbit was the animal that played the most important part in altering the course of British history.

Enough of history, and on to the rabbit, its ways and habits. First, the rabbit is a largomorph, a close cousin to the rodents. Its teeth and skeletal structure are similar to the typical rodent, as are its habits and reproduction pattern. Its breeding rate is indeed phenomenal. In past times, it rivalled the rat as the champion breeder of the animal kingdom, and its very name became synonymous with fecundity. On a 1,000-acre estate in Lincolnshire, 10,000 head of rabbit were once killed

113

in a year, and Simpson, in his book *Rabbit Warrens that Pay*, believes that at least 50,000 rabbits would be taken on this amount of land. Marchington, in his estimable and erudite book, *Pugs and Drummers*, notes that a large and well-run warren in Thetford produced an average of 28,886 rabbits each year. On land unfit for agriculture, wasteland, scrubland, tangled degenerate alder woods and so forth, the raising of rabbits as a cash crop may well have been commendable. Elsewhere, it was a devil of a nuisance.

Before the rabbit came to be regarded as Public Enemy No.2, second only to the rat, it was customary to bring in new blood to improve the size of the average rabbit in the warren. Silver greys (a domestic rabbit) were commonly turned loose to mate with the wild strains and produce whoppers of 4 pounds in weight. Guy Smith, in his *Ferreting and Trapping for Amateur Gamekeepers*, mentions that Belgian hares were turned loose on one estate, and that, to his surprise, they bred with wild rabbits. Belgian hares are, in fact, simply a breed of tame rabbit and are in no way related to hares. Haagerdoorn, in his magnificently inaccurate *Animal Breeding*, a wonderfully interesting but very unscientific book by today's standards, states that hares will interbreed with rabbits quite readily. This has been put to the test under laboratory conditions and found not to be the case. In fact, it seems unlikely that even brown and blue hares will mate together, let alone brown hares and rabbits.

There was good reason why warreners and land-owners should turn loose silver-grey rabbits on the shoots. The price of rabbits at the turn of the century was around the 2s. 6d. (12½p) a pair mark, and skins found a ready market in the felt-making trade. Wild rabbit pelts are more suitable for felt making than are those of tame domesticated rabbit pelts, for the ever-present urine in the typical warren alters the pelt's chemical structure sufficiently to make it more suitable for tanning. The silver grey x wild rabbit pelt was larger, more dense, and very little different in colour from the agouti-coloured wild rabbit skins. At the turn of the century, wild hybrid silver-grey pelts fetched about a penny halfpenny (the equivalent of just under ½p in metric money) apiece, not considerable by today's standards, perhaps, but when hauls of 10,000 rabbits were taken annually, it could be a considerable return. I should also like to mention that 1½d. was not to be sniffed at in those days. My grandfather, as fecund, perhaps, as the rabbit itself, reared twelve children, and his weekly wage in 1900 was 12s. 3d. (just over 60p).

Against the economic value of the rabbit, however, we must set its nuisance value. On good agricultural land it could be a heller, particularly if it was good agricultural land that bordered a rough patch whose owner was running a warren. Rabbits are no respecters of property, and they have created havoc on agricultural land. Sheail, in his *Rabbits and Their History*, states that in 1845 one farmer estimated that rabbits cost him £180 to £200 each year, and that another committed suicide while shouting, 'Rabbits have killed me.' No more lunatic, perhaps, than Moore, who said, 'Silly sheep are devouring men.' Rabbits have put many farmers into bankruptcy.

On the subject of sheep, it used to be estimated that between five and ten rabbits could eat as much as a sheep, but it was not the amount they ate that caused the havoc. Rabbits are choosy feeders, nibbling pieces here and there, causing the deaths of many plants and trees. Furthermore, the rabbit defecates in certain definite patches, depositing up to 360 pellets a day and a large amount of urine to go with the faeces. Land around these patches becomes decidedly acidic, and good grasses and fodder plants give way to spurry and useless herbage. The Ministry of Agriculture, prior to 1953, issued dozens of photographs showing rabbit damage in corn and other crops, and there was a staggering amount of depredation done by this rodent.

Things change, however, sometimes for the better, though more often than not for the worse – particularly if man has a hand in it. I suppose things began to go wrong, at least initially, in 1787, when some damned fool introduced rabbits into Australia, and in 1859, when twenty-four were turned loose in Barwon Park, Victoria, supposedly to assuage the homesickness of English immigrants who longed for just a reminder of home. The rabbit proved a rather unsuitable reminder, however, for the marsupial (pouched animal) predators could do little to control this virile, sexy English import, and the twenty-four in Victoria became millions in double-quick time. The rabbit turned into the all-time nuisance, a juggernaut impossible to stop. Rabbits became the reason for bankruptcy, the living of pest controllers and an inspiration for folk-song writers. 'The Sydney Rabbit Sales' was a popular folk-song in England in the early 1900s, but a cause for some bitterness among the settlers who found themselves penniless through the havoc of the humble bunny, their despair probably heightened by Harting, who, in 1898, wrote in his book *The Rabbit*: 'What is certain is that we shall always have him, not only in sufficiency, but in superabundance.' Good old Harting, oft-quoted delightful reading, and, as usual, inaccurate to a degree. Things were about to change, and the situation in Australia probably provided the impetus for such change.

In 1898, a disease of South American rabbits, caused by a virus, was isolated by the Italian bacteriologist, Giuseppe Sanarelli, and labelled myxomatosis, a name that must have sounded like the tocsin for the European rabbit. The native South American bunnies in which it was found were relatively immune to the disease, an immunity brought about by a few million years of contact, and when infected they developed swellings and the usual myxi symptoms, but recovered more often than not. A slightly different species is the South American rabbit, but the potential use of the disease was not overlooked by those who jokingly call themselves biologists and who are often a million times more destructive than the hunter they decry. Germ warfare was nothing new in South America. Pizarro, troubled by forest Indians, turned loose smallpox victims into the jungle, thereby wiping out many tribes, both hostile and friendly. Perhaps South America has a heritage of such things, but it was not long before scientists, more concerned with micro-organisms than with suffering, turned their curious eyes to Australia, where their germs might possibly find a rich harvest of distress in small creatures.

Aragao, a biologist in Brazil, had discovered that the disease could be spread by flies and even mosquitoes, and soon the Australian authorities were becoming interested in the devilish virus. In 1936, Charles Martin of Cambridge produced a virulent strain that wiped out two entire colonies of forty-four and fifty-five wild rabbits. Well done, Sir Charles, the disease was now well and truly on its way to Australia. Yet somehow anything concerned with a virus, the smallest, most mindless of organisms, seems to get out of hand, particularly when aided by another mindless creature – namely, the biologist.

A quick look at the consequences of the South American virus is now called for, though for most countrymen it is unnecessary to describe the symptoms it produces. The fleas which carry the bug only breed on pregnant rabbits, and when they leave their dying host, biting and infecting their new victim, the incubation period is from five to seven days. At first there is only a watery discharge from the eyes of the victim as the tear ducts become slightly inflamed. Within a few days, however, the eyelids begin to swell until the rabbit's eyes are sealed and it is, to all intents and purposes, blind. Swellings filled with gelatinous mess now appear around the ears, anus and genitals of the creature, and death usually comes within eighteen days of the infection. As a rule, few get this far, for their impaired reflexes and eyesight make them easy prey to stoats, badgers or foxes, and even large rats have been seen devouring still living diseased rabbits. Unpleasant and bordering on the macabre as the disease certainly is, there are still certain scientists who believe it causes no pain. May I stress that this is a belief, not a scientific fact. That badly affected animals appear to bask in the sun right up to the point of death, and even try to mate, as Locksley observes, only a few hours from death, does nothing to prove the disease is painless. The reason for the apparently leisurely basking in sun is probably hypothermia (a drop in body temperature), which anyone who has

116

been lost in a snowstorm will know is a particularly unpleasant prospect of death. Citing the mating act just prior to death does not stand up to scrutiny either. Groundsel, a simple weed, will, when denied water, seed in a desperate but futile attempt to procreate before extinction. I am still convinced that myxomatosis is a horrendous death, and that comments to the contrary are made simply to allay the conscience which pricks mankind.

In Australia, after several attempts to introduce the virus, the bug finally caught hold, carried from rabbit to rabbit by mosquitoes – in fact, any bloodsucking insect from tics to midges can transfer the virus. By 1952, there were literally millions of rotting carcasses in New South Wales and Victoria, and the death of this immigrant produced an increase in agricultural produce, the estimated value of which was £50 million per annum. Myxomatosis was here to stay, the Australian press gleefully reported. Perhaps it would have been best for it to stay in Australia. Sadly, it did not.

In June 1952, Dr Armand Delille, whose Hippocratic oath obviously included no clause concerning rabbits, obtained a highly virulent dose of myxoma virus from Switzerland. Some, seeking to excuse his actions, say that his estate was plagued with rabbits, but this is no real justification. Perhaps to rid his estate of rabbits, perhaps merely to while away a few hours of retirement, he inoculated two rabbits with the virus and turned them loose in his estate near Paris. To his delight, the virus wiped out his entire rabbit population within a month. French authorities say that the mortality rate could have been as high as 99 per cent. Once started, it is difficult to stop the disease, and, as a scientist, Delille must have known this. The result of his playing at God was catastrophic. By 1956, 90 per cent of the European rabbit population had bitten the dust and the ecology of the Continent had changed drastically, if not irrevocably. Locksley believes that the rabbit will never return to its former numbers, even after it has become immune to myxomatosis. Given a chance I am sure it will, but immunity to such a disease takes some time, even for the fecund little rabbit.

There is little doubt that it was deliberately introduced into our own country, for in October 1953 an outbreak was recorded in Kent, and a fortnight later an outbreak occurred in Sussex. The authorities, who had watched the havoc caused on the Continent, sought to enclose the infected areas with rabbit-proof netting, but this has never really been effective at stopping rabbits, let alone a virus, and 1954 saw infected rabbits appearing in every part of Britain.

Without doubt men helped to spread this disease by deliberately introducing infected rabbits into certain districts. I know this to be true, for, to my everlasting shame, I was one of those who supplied infected rabbits to farmers. In 1955, I was in the middle of an unhappy two years doing National Service, and spent a leave with a girl friend and her parents at Innsworth, Gloucester. There had been an outbreak of disease near the village, and somehow or the other her uncle asked me to provide a few infected rabbits to take to his farm near Kirkby Lonsdale in Westmorland. I borrowed a ferret and nets, and obliged, little realizing the horror the virus would cause. I produced ten watery-eyed rabbits from a near-by farm, and he took them north with him. That area of north-west England around the border between Westmorland and Lancashire was denuded of rabbits within a year.

I will not seek to justify my actions by the fact that I was earning £1 a week in the forces and the tip earned from my ten infected rabbits came in handy. I was totally ignorant of the consequences of my action, and am not in any way consoled by the fact that the disease would have reached the area anyway. I hope Armand Delille experienced pangs of conscience about his experiment. I certainly had sleepless nights over my actions. May I seek to salve my troubled conscience by saying that where Delille was a retired doctor, I was merely a callow lad of eighteen, ignorant and sure of myself as only eighteen-year-olds can be. Perhaps the difference between us is that whereas we were both scientists, I am a hunter, and the true hunter is by instinct an ecologist, regarding the countryside as a larder to be used in times of need, but never emptied. Again, perhaps, I do not have the conscience-free mind of the true scientist.

So myxomatosis came to our green and somewhat troubled land, and with the passing of the rabbit, various ecological changes occurred. Foxes left the countryside, now denuded of rabbit, to feed on rats and garbage in the town refuse piles. Buzzards had one glorious year feeding on the dying rabbits, and then became rare when the food supply dried up. Stoats – well, they became a rarity anyway. While the rabbit was an intruder, an invader of our land, its predators had had 2,000 years to become accustomed to his face, and once he was gone the balance of nature was again disturbed. While the Ministry of Agriculture became a battleground for those who thought we should stop the spread of the disease and those who wanted to help spread it, the face of the countryside altered.

Not all the rabbits died, though it was a near thing. One in a hundred survived, perhaps – some getting over the infection, some eccentric enough to nest in gorse and undergrowth far from the warrens which held the bloodsucking, disease-spreading fleas. Slowly, but slowly, the population of rabbits rose, but every few years a fresh outbreak of the disease would clear out an entire district. Infected does who had recovered passed on their immunity to their young via the colostrum, or first milk, but it was an immunity that was short-lived: three to twelve weeks' worth of antibodies in the bloodstream able to fight off the myxoma infection, and then every rabbit for himself, so to speak. Rodents and largomorphs alike, while not being particularly intelligent, are simply the most resilient creatures on God's earth. It may take a hundred years to develop immunity to this disease, but I am confident that the rabbit will do so in the end, and will survive. By that time, I am also confident, mankind will have developed something even nastier for the poor rabbit.

Do you find this an unpleasant start to a chapter? Well, perhaps it is, but things have changed since Harting and Simpson, and it is necessary to assess the problems which the rabbit has experienced before going on to describe his breeding habits and how to hunt him. I doubt if these two oft-quoted writers would recognize our rabbitless land should they return from their graves to view it. The present-day rabbit, its habits and numbers, have certainly changed greatly since the halcyon days of the 1900s.

Now for the breeding habits of the rabbit. Like their domesticated relatives, wild rabbits become sexually mature at four to five months old, and at this age they also mate. Young are produced after a thirty-one-day gestation period, and the doe builds a nest made of fur plucked from her own chest to cover them. Unlike the hare, the rabbit is born blind and naked, but growth is very rapid to compensate for early disadvantages. A curious fact about rodents and largomorphs is that they are highly fertile within hours of the birth of their young, so it is more than likely that, in a well-balanced colony, the does mate on the same day as parturition occurs.

Temperature is all-important in the breeding cycle of the rabbit. In years when Britain experiences the mildest winters, the rabbit will breed the year round, but in freezing winters, the does are reluctant to mate until late spring. Domestic rabbits will usually refuse to mate in winter, unless kept in specially heated or insulated sheds, as are the commercial herds of rabbits. On 27 December 1977, I ferreted a sheltered bank on the Dyatt estate at Lichfield, and took a doe who had kindled only a few days earlier – sufficient to say, my ferret made carnage among the babes. In 1976, however, the same estate had yielded March rabbits who were not in kindle. Bush rabbits – a dubious strain who live above ground, building nests in deep cover – probably come into season only when the warm days of spring arrive. It is also of interest to note that tame does who lose their litters through some mishap are usually ready to receive the buck immediately, and if she is denied mating, the results can be a little traumatic, for the doe may refuse mating for months afterwards. It seems likely

119

that the constant cycle of breeding is rarely varied in a well-balanced warren.

Rabbits feed out from late afternoon until early morning. Locksley, whose *Private Life of the Rabbit* is for the rabbit what Lorenz's work is to jackdaws, says that the rabbit feeds out at night. Certainly the rabbit is found out in great numbers at night, though Marchington questions whether they are simply out to feed. Night-time offers security to the rabbit, and he will feed far from his burrow; but dawn, or early dusk, will find him only a few feet from the warren, ever wary and quick to flash to safety should danger threaten.

To catch rabbits out feeding (lamping apart, for that is an entirely different technique) is quite difficult, and the hauls are invariably small. The twilight is, perhaps, the best time to run them, and many dogs adjust to this half-light very well. I have seen many lurchers run rabbits that I have overlooked in the twilight, and catch the rabbits, too, I might add, but whatever the time, without the aid of ferrets or other devices to expel the rabbits from their holes, hauls of rabbit are bound to be small in daylight hunting, and frankly are very hard earned.

One method of persuading rabbits to leave the sanctuary of the burrow is the process of stinking out, or inserting foul-smelling substances in the hole. Paraffin, creosote, even waste oil is suitable, but the best of all is the chemical known as Renardine. This, placed in holes some days before one intends to hunt the area, will ensure that only the most terrified rabbit will be underground. There is a problem, though. The use of stinking out is obvious, but any rabbits not taken are scattered around the area and reluctant to breed again in the foul-smelling lairs. Paraffin smells clear quickly, but Renardine seems to persist for months. It is a little unsporting, perhaps, but a good way of getting rabbits to stay above ground. It is as well to remember that a rabbit will, when hard-pressed, dive into its earth, even if it is filled with the most pungent of substances, so stinking out as an aid to hunting has its limitations. If the hunter does not adopt the use of stinking out, he must therefore expect small hauls of rabbits. To increase the haul to any great extent, he will need to work his lurcher in conjunction with ferrets.

Ferreting for Rabbits

It is rather sad that this valiant and useful creature has become the most misunderstood joke animal. I have grown virtually too ashamed to own up to keeping ferrets, as the almost inevitable question seems to be, 'Do you put them down your trousers?' I dislike such daft exhibitionism intensely, as well as the idiots who practise it. Yet, the ferret, in spite of the stupid jokes made about him, is a priceless ally to the rabbit hunter and the traditional companion of the poacher and his lurchers. The deadly combination of ferret, lurcher and man, defying authority to poach game, has been the subject of folk-stories and folk-song for generations. Steeleye Span, the electronic folk group who include among their recordings the folk-song, 'Dogs and Ferrets', have done much to restore the popularity of the old songs. It is a pretty tune, but the words are most inaccurate, for they go: 'I keep my dogs and ferrets to catch the hares that feed at night.' Either the song is a little out of kilter, or I have been keeping the wrong type of ferret. It is impossible for a ferret to aid in the night poaching of hares, and though I have used ferrets to flush them from the drains and earths into which they have dived when hard-pressed by dogs, it is the rabbit that is the traditional and logical quarry of the ferret.

Two years ago there was a scarcity of books on ferrets, and all one had to work on was a superb BFSS pamphlet by Jack Ivester Lloyd, well written and crammed with detail, but recently there has been a spate of books on ferrets and ferreting. I shall not therefore touch on the history, origins and breeding of the ferret, but move straight on to the use of the lurcher in the role of a ferreting dog, or of a dog to assist the rabbiter in his work with ferrets.

Quite simply, the ferret is put to ground to panic the rabbit into bolting. He is then either taken by nets, or shot, or coursed to the lurcher. The lurcher owner must therefore make up his mind what he wants: (a) either a ferret to flush rabbits to be coursed by his lurcher – a very sporting, exciting, but decidedly unprofitable business, since most of the rabbits will escape, particularly if several bolt simultaneously, as they often do in the first days of autumn; or (b) a lurcher to assist the ferreter with his nets – that is, to catch the rabbits that somehow or other manage to escape from the nets or holes that are unnetted through being overlooked.

Whatever the lurcher owners wants of his dog and ferret team, one thing is certain: he will not wish to have his lurcher kill the ferret. The first task is thus to break the lurcher to ferret, to make the dog understand that the ferret is an ally, not a creature to be hurt. This is ridiculously simple if one starts with the lurcher as a puppy, but a bit more difficult if the dog is an adult before being trained to ferret. Do remember that, valiant as he is, a ferret is most unlikely to survive even the merest nip from an adult lurcher, so if one has bought a grown dog (a mistake, reader, I assure you once again, a decided mistake), then great care will be needed to break him to ferret. The task becomes

121

doubly difficult if the lurcher's previous owner has ever allowed the dog to kill a ferret – a fact that you are unlikely to be told at the time of the purchase. Start, therefore, with a puppy.

Breaking a puppy, particularly a sensitive sight-hound puppy, to ferret is quite simple. It consists of placing the puppy near the ferret, preferably a veteran hob who is used to putting puppies in their place, and chiding the puppy for any violence or aggression shown towards the ferret. If the puppy is quite young, aggression towards the ferret is quickly curbed by the ferret itself, for a large hob, preferably an old mean liner, will soon show a puppy that ferrets can be unpleasant if attacked. Mutual respect is fairly essential in a dog/ferret relationship, and I have seen many ferrets come out of a warren and nip a dog. This certainly doesn't foster good relations, so as soon as the dog is broken to ferret, I suggest that the ferreter should start with a very young ferret as a hunting companion for the dog.

As soon as the puppy realizes that the ferret is not for killing, it will be good sound sense to allow great familiarity between both, and allow them to play together when you are cleaning out the ferret cage. A puppy and a young ferret will get up to some amazing capers together, cavorting and wrestling and generally acting almost insanely, but this is all an essential part of training. Great familiarity is needed when a dog is required to distinguish between a ferret and a rabbit, particularly when the rabbit is exploding from its warren at about 24 miles an hour. Allow them to get used to each other, to drink milk from the same saucer, though I should add that I would be a little reluctant to allow them to feed from the same dish, since both dogs and ferrets are somewhat possessive about meat and a nasty incident could arise through food jealousy. Don't worry about the stupid way the pair act when they are playing together. When the time comes, both will settle down to work soon enough. Your task will be not to stop them playing together, but merely to prevent incidents that could sever the relationship between the two little hunters.

Which breeds of lurcher make suitable ferreting dogs? Well, there are many, the only criterion being that they should not be too large. The stately deerhound/greyhound hybrid might be deadly on hare, running the animal literally into the ground after a mile course, but it would not galvanize into action quickly enough to snap up a rabbit as it sped between hole and hedge – no more than a twenty-yard dash, perhaps. A small, nimble lurcher is the job for the ferreter, and this is where the whippet lurcher comes into play. Whippet hybrids, or small greyhound hybrids, make the most useful ferreting dogs, preferably with a bit of coat for protection, for rabbits are apt to play rather dirty and dive into cover as soon as they bolt, so that a dog needs some protection when he has to dash into brambles after the quarry. Whippet/Bedlington hybrids seem to be the most popular ferreting dogs, combining the speed of the whippet and the gutsy nature of the Bedlington. Similarly, small collie lurchers, either whippet/collie crosses, perhaps using racing types of whippet as the base stock, or small greyhound/collie hybrids, make ideal dogs, for not only are they good in rough, but they can also be easily trained to any task and do not have the trend to stubborn impetuosity of the Bedlington hybrid.

When it comes to hunting the dog and ferret combination, choose easily netted warrens to start with. Newly opened settes are ideal since, should your ferret lie up here, he can easily be dug out. Autumn and winter are the times to start training, once the cold period of the year has brought about a cessation in the rabbit's breeding cycle. Allow the dog to wander free and find the earths, but prevent him from scratching at the burrows, or, worse still, snuffling down them, so literally telling the rabbit of the perils that await him should he bolt – and he will probably decline to bolt once he knows about the welcoming committee that awaits him above ground. Restrain your dog gently, however, and then start to assess the warren and quietly clear away undergrowth and brush that might tangle the nets when the rabbits hit them. Now is the time when that basic obedience, scorned by men who are unable to teach it, comes into its own. Get your dog to sit while you net the warren. A dog wandering about, uprooting nets, causing tangles and bedlam, is insufferable. He must settle down close at hand and watch the warrens.

The brush is now cleared, the nets pegged down. Station your dog in position, well clear of the burrow mouth but close enough to grab a bolting rabbit if it casts the nets and escapes. Dogs should be made to sit on early forays, but on later hunts, when they know what is expected of them, most will stand with a cat-like stealth above the hole, quivering with excitement and anticipation. Be sure that the dog is not visible to any rabbit about to creep out. If he sees the dog, the chances are that he will creep back. Thus the dog must remain within easy reach of the warren, but out of view.

Once the dog is positioned and nets placed, it is time to put the ferret to work. Place him to the mouth of the earth, but do not ram him down. Let him sniff and savour the scent of rabbit around the outside of the hole before he crawls in. Listen carefully, and you will hear the sound of bumping as the rabbit kicks off the ferret and gallops around the set, trying to bewilder the adversary tracking him in the darkness of the warren with the remorselessness of a bloodhound. Watch the dog: his ears are keener than yours, so the sound of the activity below ground will have more meaning for him. It will also excite him into taking a more active part in the hunt. Restrain him with a gesture of the hand, not a shout. Silence is all-important in ferreting.

Suddenly a rabbit, no longer able to face the fury that has beset him below ground, hits the nets – but the time has come for maximum restraint. Hold your dog, or fix him with a hand gesture while you dispatch the rabbit, quickly and painlessly, replacing your nets as before. Another hits your nets – restrain your dog again. If he once interferes with a netted rabbit, he will create red ruin in the nets before you are able to stop him. Another is netted, but before you have time to replace your nets, yet another has bolted through the space and is fleeing for the sanctuary of the hedge. Now urge on your lurcher – the time for restraint is over. He runs the fleeing rabbit, in and out of the hedgerow, before snapping it up and returning it to hand. The ferret emerges as the dog deposits the rabbit in your hand.

Take care, this is a moment of potential crisis, for a dispute over the rightful ownership of the dead rabbit could result in a slain ferret and a dog useless in the sport for which he was intended. Once a lurcher has

First rabbit, albeit a diseased one. 'Merle' at 6½ months old.

124

killed a ferret, he will be very difficult to break to them again. Therefore watch the bottle-brush tail of the ferret. Allow him to grab the dead rabbit and drag it around for a moment, but not back into the warren, where he will eat it in peace and lie up. Once his fury has cooled and his tail is its normal shape again, pick him up and box or bag him.

It may be weeks before your dog learns the difference between a netted rabbit and one that has bolted and is fair game, but there are no short cuts to success in the training of a ferreting dog. Training such a dog is, indeed, a task, but more than a task – a challenge which those content only to slip a long dog at a fleeing hare will never appreciate. Ferreting is wonderfully educating to both dog and man, and no other sport can teach a man bushcraft so well.

Rabbit warrens are highly cosmopolitan dwellings as to their inhabitants, and cats, rats, foxes and stoats are often bolted by ferrets from the self-same earths as rabbits. In the beginning, you will judge whether an earth is inhabited by various signs: a well-worn path to the earth would suggest it was inhabited, recently excavated earth and leaves will also indicate the presence of rabbits at home. Droppings in the mouth of an earth bespeak that the warren is used as a playhole and that the inhabited warren is maybe twenty or thirty yards away. Gradually, however, the dog will learn his trade and your need for bushcraft will become less, for the lurcher will tell you whether the rabbit is at home far better than can your personal study of rabbit spoor. Your judgement is fallible. If he is left to his own devices and not encouraged to false mark, your dog's nose will supplant your bushcraft. If properly trained, he will stand pointing an inhabited earth, quivering with excitement like a pointer at a field trial.

There is only one way to bring a dog up to this standard, and that is sheer hard work. He must constantly accompany you on ferreting trips, and you will learn his idiosyncrasies at the same time as he learns yours. One lurcher I know, a mongrel with a good proportion of whippet and perhaps a dash of terrier, will touch the earth with a paw and whine piteously if rats are present, and though he will snap up rabbits with the best of them, he lets rats and stoats slip through the mesh of the net unhurt.

As time goes on, your dog will become a priceless acquisition. Not only will he mark the inhabited earth and snap up the rabbits that have slipped your slovenly placed nets, but if your ferret should kill a rabbit and lie up eating the carcass below ground, a dog will often stand above the dining ferret, indicating its whereabouts as efficiently as could any electronic device. All one has to do is dig to retrieve both rabbit and ferret.

As I have emphasized, these skills are not easily acquired and it will take years to train a dog to such perfection, but if your puppy is taught correctly, he will certainly learn the art of working with ferrets. Should you try to buy such a dog, properly trained by a skilful trainer, no one will sell you one. Nor will you sell yours once you reflect on how long it has taken you to perfect the skill of ferreting with dog and lurcher. There is only one way to obtain such a paragon: you must train it yourself, and it will be a long, hard task. There are no short cuts in the creation of a first-class ferreting dog.

The Hare

Here is a creature worthy of study, and, unlike the rabbit, it is a true
native of Britain. The Romans found the tribes of East Anglia worship-
ping a hare goddess, and few creatures are as worthy of worship as the
hare, I am sure. Two types of hare exist in Britain (or three, if you count
the Irish hare). The blue hare is a sluggish, smaller, creature than the
brown hare, and it is of the brown hare that we will speak throughout
this chapter, for the blue hare is confined to Scotland and the Isle of
Man and is not the sporting beast which his southern cousin rep-
resents – and, reader, dazzled as you are by advertisements which
blandly state 'This dog will kill four out of four hares', a sporting beast he
is, a god-almighty athlete whose very muscle structure and natural
history bespeaks the untruth in such advertisements. 'Four out of four',
indeed. What superb hyperbole, what a shocking lie! Such dogs are
seldom born, and if they should be they are never, ever sold.

You dispute my statement? Let us turn to science rather than sales
talk. Let us not eulogize on speed, but rather resort to dissection to
assess the hare's prowess. Skin a hare and examine its body. His hind

legs and the muscles concerned with propulsion are huge. The muscles are knotted lumps, capable of hurling him forward, and one third of his entire weight is concerned with propulsion. Indeed, it is a saying among gipsy folk that a hare's hind leg is a meal for a man, albeit a hard-earned meal. Dig now into the muscles that bind the hind legs to the spine: they are massive lumps of connecting tissue, capable of hurling the hare sideways in mid-flight, capable of allowing him to turn in his own length, to double back on himself and confound his pursuer.

Cut through the membranous diaphragm, the layer that divides the thorax, or chest cavity, from the guts. Look inside the chest cavity at the lungs. They are out of proportion to a beast this size, ridiculous in their hugeness, but definitely purposeful – lungs that will allow the maximum intake of oxygen, the greatest release of energy; lungs of a size that are the hallmark of stamina. Cut deeper still and, marvel of marvels, come to the heart: four times the size of a rabbit heart, the size of a baby's fist; a massive pumping machine capable of pumping blood at an enormous rate, capable of allowing the animal to run for ever, it would seem. Anatomically, the hare is a marvel, a beast of legendary stamina, legendary speed, built only to run, the athlete of the animal world. The Indians say of a large type of black buck that, on the day of his birth, a man can catch him, on the second day only a swift hound, but on the third day only God himself. Perhaps their species is faster than our hare, but on the day when the Almighty allocated speed and stamina, grit and agility, the hare must have been close to the front of the queue.

Do you still hanker to believe in the veracity of our advertisement? Here, then, is the final test. Examine the hare's lifestyle and discover the reason for his survival, even his increase in number, for if such paragons of dogs were common there would be no hares. Unlike the rabbit, he has no holes into which he can bolt in times of trouble, for like the biblical Son of Man, he has no place to hide his head. His defence is flight, and throughout the ages the weak among his kind, the sufferers of cardiac or pulmonary disorders, those unable to outpace the pursuers, have gone to the wall. Only the fleet and agile survived. A million or maybe two million years of breeding – selected breeding of the toughest school – have gone into this beast. He has had an aeon of time to complete the diversification of type, the difference between hare and rabbit. He has been around since before man, and he has survived the hardest treatment. Poets have eulogized on his speed in tongues older than Sanskrit, but man, for as long as he has possessed the sight hound, has harried the hare remorselessly. Now view the advertisement in the cold light of reason. 'This dog will kill four out of four hares.' If such a dog existed it must be valued beyond price, and its owner would sooner trade his family, home or both than part with such a beast.

Little or no research on the brown hare has been done in Britain. To the sportsman, he is a creature to be shot or coursed and often left on the field rather than taken home to be eaten. Hare meat is dissimilar to rabbit. Tegner, in his neatly compiled *Wild Hares*, makes reference to the researches of scientists in Russia, Finland and Germany, but while these may be of some use in helping us to understand the hare, it is fair to point out that it does not necessarily follow that the behaviour of the hare of the Continent is identical to that of the British hare.

Mating, at any rate, commences early in the year, and the jack hare is very savage towards intruding males. I have seen several grim teeth and hind-leg fights that have lasted a full minute or so before supremacy was established and the loser limped away. Millais states that captive hares fight to the death, but it is foolish to assume that they will do so in the wild. Lorenz states that, providing escape is possible, few creatures will continue a battle with their own kind unto death. Perhaps the only creature that will pursue a conflict well past the stage where his opponent has submitted is man, as he is probably motivated (made neurotic, would be more correct) by his crowded world.

The gestation period of the hare is considerably longer than that for the rabbit, forty-eight days as opposed to thirty-one, and the sixteen-day difference is important, for the hare is born fully furred and able to run from the moment of birth. (The rabbit, with its correspondingly shorter gestation period, is born blind, naked and helpless, but in the protection of a burrow.) The leveret, or young hare, is born in a roughly made nest in a wind-swept field. Yet while they can run from the time of their birth, most will lie quite still when approached, preferring to be overlooked rather than chased. Hares produce maybe four or five young in a litter, depositing them in various fields, probably in the hope that at least one will survive, and suckling them by turn in the night and early morning. Perhaps two litters are born a year, but, again, little research has been done on the British hare. Amateur naturalists like Cowper, the poet, have kept them in captivity in a walled garden, and one of his lived for twelve years, but studies of any creature under such circumstances is hardly equivalent to studying it in the wild. It should also be noted that Cowper was a gentle poet subject to periods of mental disturbance, not a scientist trained in the observation of the habits of wild animals. I can only say that leverets I have seen in captivity, particularly any jack hares (males), were invariably too savage to handle, and that, in common with all wild animals, hares make unsuitable domestic pets.

The size of the quarry is an important subject in a chapter on hares, particularly in a book for lurchermen, for coursing men are like fishermen and rarely weigh their catches and so tall stories abound. Tegner quotes 8 pounds as an average weight, though a survey I conducted in about 1975 arrived at an average weight a little over $7\frac{1}{2}$ pounds. Thirteen-pound hares have been recorded (they seem to be caught daily by a majority of lurchermen), but those are very rare indeed. One hare which I found dead, as a result of a motor-car accident, in Norwich, weighed a fraction over 11 pounds, this being the largest hare I have ever seen.

This, then, is the quarry, or, viewed in the light of his athletic ability, the opponent. His only defence is flight, and rapid flight at that. When he is hard-pressed, he will dive into any pipe or rabbit warren available, and in country where hares are constantly run and pestered by hordes of men and sundry coursing dogs, he will use this tactic frequently. Green hares, or hares that are seldom, if ever, run, are loth to get to ground, but they soon learn that this is an accepted method of escape. In the district in which I live, hares get a very bad time from coursing men, so much so that it is a wonder they still abound. Most of them will put into an earth if one is available. Keith Quimby, who 'runs' the district frequently, tells two stories of hares going to ground, one in a narrow pipe, from which it was flushed by a terrier – after, I might add, a tremendous scuffle, for the hare weighed 9 pounds and so did the terrier; and one in a disused rabbit warren, from where it was flushed by a huge hob ferret belonging to me. Hares in pipes can give a small dog a very bad time, for not only do they bite quite badly, but a kick from a hind leg can cause severe damage. Brian Vesey-Fitzgerald mentions that it was with great difficulty that he once managed to hold a live hare. On one occasion I watched a hare put to ground by beagles, and returned to ferret it an hour later. My jill ferret was quite keen to get out from the warren after her first encounter with the beast, which could kick like a mule. More often than not, however, ferrets succeed in driving out a hare more easily than they would a rabbit, for a hare gone to ground is in alien surroundings and is keen to be away into the open again. On reflection, perhaps the words of the folk-song, 'Dogs and Ferrets', which I quoted earlier (page 0-00), may have a ring of truth to them.

In the wild, the hare has few enemies, though leveret mortality rate is fairly high. Crows, foxes and even jays are reputed to attack leverets, as are gulls, who are formidable birds with a great deal of courage and aggression. Foxes snap up newly born leverets quite readily, though Nature, wishing to preserve the hare, ensures that the babies have very little scent, whereas the adult is quite heavily scented. Within a matter of days, however, the newly born leveret is able to outstrip most ground pursuers, and few birds will contemplate an attack on even a half-grown leveret, though eagles can, and do, take hares, and with great ease. Even captive trained eagles find the taking of a hare well within their capabilities, but the hare has few foes that can come near to catching him once he is fully grown. He sleeps cat-napping, half-sleeping, half-waking, galvanizing into action the moment danger threatens. Few hares are taken by foxes, weasels or stoats, no matter what the nursery natural history books may tell us.

Before we come to the coursing of the hare, it is wise to mention that beagling is a very successful, if lengthy, method of taking hares. Of course, no beagle or harrier could outrun a hare in a fair course, and the hunt becomes a grinding war of attrition as the beagles hunt up, lose him, then find him again, hunting him by scent alone most of the time. Some hunts continue for hours and are quite savage, since the hare may be practically dead from exhaustion before the beagles manage to seize him. Beagling is a fairly brutal form of hunting, and while coursing, which involves a fairly short, sharp and easily finished form of hunting, arouses the wrath of the public, it is strange that beagling rarely does. Perhaps the anti-bloodsport fraternity are reluctant to run with the beagles all day to protest their case, though from the antics seen at a recent Waterloo Cup, most seem to be pretty energetic. It has always baffled me as to why beagling passes unnoticed under the very noses of the anti-bloodsport people. The most logical reason, of course, is that they are the most misinformed bunch of individuals one could hope to meet, being motivated by unreasonable passions rather than any real study of the activity they are sabotaging.

So to the coursing of our quarry, or at least our attempt to do so, for it is a task more easily said than done. To hunt hare with any degree of success, a lurcher needs to be well grown. Fifteen months old is not too great an age to try a dog at hare, and later, perhaps, is more advisable. The reasons are many. First, the hare is the athlete of the animal kingdom and a lurcher puppy is ridiculously outmatched by such a quarry. Thus a gutsy dog will try hard at his hare, straining heart, lungs, muscles and diaphragm. Strained respiratory tracts are frequently encountered in lurchers which are tried either too hard or too frequently at hares. Damage is usually permanent. The term 'blown' is applied to a dog who has had his heart, lungs or diaphragm damaged as a result of the severity of a course.

Another reason for allowing a puppy to develop properly before coursing it at hare is the problem known as 'opening up'. Here the dog is outmatched by a hare and, in despair at seeing its prey escape, utters a short, sharp bark. It is a habit that is hard to cure, and not only does it give the game away for the poacher, it also alerts every beast for miles around. Whippet-blooded dogs, thwarted at hares and suchlike, are notorious for 'opening up'. Once it has become a habit, I'm afraid the dog will rarely chase without giving tongue. This is why advertisements for lurchers always stress the word 'silent' in their appraisal of a dog. 'Opening up' is a cardinal sin for any poaching man, and is usually a fault of premature entering. Any good coursing man gives his dog ample time to develop before allowing him to course a hare. One hears stories of puppies taking hare with consummate ease. Treat such tales with suspicion, take them with a pinch of salt – a block or so, I would suggest.

Early success is very important in any form of dog training. A terrier that has had frequent failures at rat hunting is often loth to hunt rats. Likewise a lurcher that fails repeatedly against hares will often not give its best during courses as it develops a sort of canine inferiority complex about being overmatched. Easy courses (are any courses against hares easy?) will be essential for the young lurcher if he is to gain confidence in himself and become a good hare courser. Walsh advises slipping the sapling lurcher on a hare that has been coursed by an older dog – if possible, a course that has exhausted the hare. Ideal, but a little unsporting? Well, any form of entering to quarry needs to be a little unsporting if one is to tilt the odds in favour of the lurcher. Myxied rabbits, blinded by the filthy blight, do not overtax the puppy, and certainly will give it confidence to try for healthy rabbits. Likewise, a tired hare is suitable opposition for a young lurcher, as yet inexperienced in catching this darting, bobbing cyclone. The chances are that he will not catch even a tired hare, but he has at least had a chance, which is more than he would have had against a fresh hare. Therefore, failing the coursing of a hare tired by another dog, a suitable method of entering might be a hare caught cat-napping in long grass, and using a close slip at that. Avoid long slips, giving the hare law, and try to aim at success, not sportsmanship, during the first runs. Time enough to be fair when the dog is catching well. Tegner estimates that only one in five hares are taken by the average entered lurcher, and this is probably a fairly high number. The chances of a puppy, or a sapling, taking a hare are extremely remote. Again, I repeat, early successes in entering any dog to quarry are essential.

As for the merits of slipping the lurcher on a hare and/or allowing him to hunt up the quarry, there are many differences of opinion. Early lurchers of the Norfolk type were certainly required to hunt up their hares and to course them, but most lurchermen today prefer to slip their dogs as they would a coursing greyhound. Both methods have their merits. Consider first the merits of slipping the dog on the hare. The advantages are, for instance, that a man's eyesight is superior to a dog's, even a sight hound's, and therefore the man is able to discern a hare at a greater distance and so to walk it up in a rather grotesque parody of stalking. Next, the man who slips the dog is able to decide whether the hare in question is suitable for coursing. When a dog is running loose, hunting up his quarry, then that is a different matter, and a lurcher will often give chase to a hare that he has not a hope in hell of catching. A slipped dog can be run on any hare the lurcherman decides.

Against running off a slip, it must be mentioned that a dog run in this manner has little to commend it over a greyhound – more stamina perhaps, but this is counter-balanced by the reduced speed of the lurcher as opposed to the greyhound. The true early lurchers, the providers for the pot, were certainly required to hunt up the quarry. A lurcher used to hunt up hare is moreover able to find the quarry should he lose it in cover or long grass, whereas the sight-hunting lurcher, run from a slip, is often baffled by the disappearance of the hare. Lastly, from the aesthetic angle, nothing looks more beautiful than a lurcher, hunting nose down, weather eye open for movement and the final coursing of the hare. Still, it is a matter of opinion. Personally, I like to watch nose work as much as a course.

Hare killing, provided the dog has speed enough, is a matter of practice. The more you hunt the dog the better he will become. Daily hunts produce an excellent hare killer, provided the hunter has sense enough not to run the dog to a state of exhaustion each day. A hare is a most testing quarry, and repeated runs at fresh hares with a dog which is obviously panting hard, flanks heaving and mouth steaming, can literally be the dog's death. Greyhounds and lurchers with a great deal of greyhound blood will usually keep trying until they drop, but the nearer one breeds to the greyhound, that is, three quarters, seven eighths greyhound, the less stamina the dog will possess, although he will certainly be fast enough for hares. At a great number of lurcher shows many lurchers are almost indistinguishable from greyhounds. Many track greyhounds even are shown as lurchers at shows. In fact, it is a joke among local lurcher judges that the only way one can judge a show and not be accused of picking out a greyhound for best in show is to make the best a rough-coated animal. At the first hint of making up a smooth-coated dog, the malcontent who has won nothing will invariably claim that the judge has 'made up' a track greyhound.

Before leaving the subject of the hare as quarry, it is of interest to mention the measures which Victorian keepers took to prevent poachers from taking hares on their land. Hare passages, or pipes, were placed under hedges to allow hares to pass easily from one field to another. Often these tunnels were large enough to allow a speeding small lurcher to enter them. These hare pipes could be death-traps for any dog, for they were frequently fitted with irregularly placed spikes which allowed the hares to pass along them but impaled any dog that entered the pipe at speed.

Victorian times were rough for the poacher and his dog, for the *nouveau riche* was inclined to treat human life quite lightly in the preservation of his game. Not only did Botany Bay and prisons of nightmare conditions await the poacher, but man-traps were often set for the unwary night operator. These traps, set near stiles, were really gin-traps of epic proportions, supposedly for simply trapping the poacher, but more often than not biting with such force as to maim the man, mangling his flesh so badly that amputation of a limb might be necessary to save the poor wretch's life. These traps, which could be equally dangerous to dog and man alike, were usually knocked up in the local blacksmith's shop, using a large gin as a guide, or better still, an antique bear-trap, though various firms in Walsall and Birmingham specialized in making such traps. In fact, most of the traps sold to early Hudson Bay trappers were made in the forges of Birmingham and Walsall.

About six years ago a Walsall foundry was demolished, and among the papers thrown out was a pattern for a man-trap-cum-bear-trap. Possessed as I am with an interest in the macabre, I set to in the school metal workshop and made a trap to the specifications in the plan. When newly made, with a steel spring in good condition, this trap could bite into a pickaxe handle making cuts half an inch deep in the wood. In 1827, man-traps were made illegal, but many keepers continued to use such traps right up to the First World War. Few people in search of game at night were willing to report their use, even when damaged by them, for a court presided over by the landed gentry would be unlikely to convict a fellow landowner who set his land with man-traps. Prior to the 1831 Game Act, moreover, day or night poaching carried savage punishments. Sentences varied from three months' hard labour for a first offence to three years' hard labour or seven years' transportation for night poaching in an armed band of three or more men. Up until 1848, licences were required to take hares by any means, from shooting to coursing. Hard times beget a particularly violent sort of poacher, and who could blame a man for fiercely resisting arrest when conviction meant seven years in Botany Bay?

I will close this section with the mention of another statute. In 1892, the Hare Preservation Act made it illegal to take hares between the months of March and July. At the time of writing, few of the punishments forged in the fire of Victoriana are observed by magistrates who, if the recent spate of poaching trials is an indication of the attitude of the

Bench, tend to treat hare coursing as something of a joke – 'the act of a naughty boy rather than a criminal offence', a barrister told me once. I am certain, however, that with the amount of money now being invested in shoots, such leniency will soon be a thing of the past. While I have no wish to see a return of the brutal Forest Laws, I feel that some recent spates of barbarism masquerading as poaching really deserve stiff punishments.

The Fox

Until a few years ago, the fox was not considered as being a creature worthy of poaching with sight hounds or lurchers, and the capture of one was usually incidental to a day's hunt – an added bonus, so to speak. Now things are different. In 1977, the fickle fur market became fox-orientated, and the pelts of the red fox, which previously sold for a matter of a pound or two, now began to fetch very high prices indeed. Silly stories are often told of the staggering price paid for fox pelts, but £15 was a realistic price for a good skin in fine condition, without damage or bad mange. Fifteen pounds is still a good price, particularly in a year when unemployment has hit an all-time record. Thus many lurchermen deliberately set out to catch fox in preference to hare, and fox poaching has become more than merely common.

So bad did the illegal taking of foxes become that, in 1977, many hunts took next to no fox, and articles decrying the killing of foxes with lurchers appeared in *Shooting Times* and other sporting periodicals. It will be interesting to see how the market in fox pelts goes in the future. Like as not, the pelts will suddenly be worth next to nothing, for a popular fur one year is decidedly out the next. Perhaps it will be for the best, though I have a sneaking suspicion that only a few years of hunting foxes on the scale of 1978 would be needed to reduce their numbers to a level where the fox became an endangered species. This is not as exaggerated as may appear when one considers that fox hunts (hunts with riders and fox hounds) are decidedly inefficient and are usually organized for entertainment rather than to reduce the fox population. The taking of foxes with lurchers, either by lamping, or by bolting them with terriers and coursing them, is a very effective method, though not a particularly sporting one, I might add.

A few details on dog/fox relationships will not come amiss here, however. First, most lurchers or sight hounds will course and catch rabbits instinctively, and one taken from a kennels without prior training will invariably find rabbits irresistible. Yet no natural enmity exists between dog and fox, and though some track greyhounds will kill foxes on sight (or any other small animal for that matter), most lurchers need to be entered to fox properly. Often lurcher owners complain that, while their dogs will chase the fox fairly readily, when the lurcher comes up on the fox they act as if somewhat bewildered, delivering a few quick but indecisive 'putts' at the fox before returning to their owner. This should not be interpreted as cowardice, but quite simply by the fact that the lurcher is somewhat bewildered as to whether or not the musky, dog-like creature it has encountered is legitimate quarry. As I have mentioned, no natural enmity exists between dog and fox.

There seems to be considerable evidence to suggest that pure-blooded sight hounds enter far more readily and far more quickly to fox than lurchers. An article appearing in the American magazine *Hunting Dogs* says the same thing about grey fox and coyote. Certainly the harebrained courage of the track or coursing greyhound is ideal for the task of taking fox, which requires little skill and also, interestingly enough, very little speed. A fox is hopelessly outmatched by the speed of any sight hound, and even a 'wastage' first-cross lurcher will find little difficulty in outpacing a fox.

The most unlikely-looking lurchers are often demon fox killers. About fifteen years ago I saw a lightly built, 24-pound whippet overtake, bowl and hold a fox, and though it was more of a duel than a hunt – a duel that could have gone either way, I should add – it does tend to show that the method of entering a dog to fox counts as much as the type of lurcher used. The most popular type of lurcher for fox coursing at the time of writing is undoubtedly the Bedlington/greyhound cross. Bull terrier/greyhound hybrids (even the heavy, ungainly specimens) run the Bedlington hybrid a close second. Pattinson had a huge wolfhound/greyhound hybrid which, though it was practically useless at hare coursing, proved to be a demon fox killer. One of the best fox-hunting lurchermen I have met, Gwyllym Hardwick of Blaengarw, used to recommend a lightly built collie dog, a rangy one if possible, mated to a greyhound, as the most suitable cross for taking foxes, particularly foxes bolted by a terrier, though I must add that Hardwick's opinion was coloured by the fact that he hunted some of the roughest terrain in Britain. Salukis and saluki hybrids can be fairly lethal with foxes, though they tend on some days to be frantic to take them and on others totally indifferent. The American coursing men invariably come out in favour of the deerhound/greyhound hybrid, though it must be mentioned that they use the fox, along with the rabbit and hare, as starters for the hunting of the more formidable and faster coyote – half-way 'twixt fox and wolf in size. As for size of dog, again one cannot be categorical, though it is reasonable to suppose that a dog below 23 inches at the shoulder may find it quite hard going to take fox regularly, and small dogs often suffer greatly through repeated encounters with foxes.

A little about the fox and his habits may well assist the would-be fox hunter. Foxes are kin blood to dogs, though their shape, particularly when skinned, and habits may suggest that they resemble cats as closely. Dogs they are, however, though contrary to country legend, dog/fox hybrids are impossible to produce. The fox is, or rather was, quite common in Britain, and though it has suffered greatly from the ravages of pelt hunters, a year of normal breeding should see the fox as common as ever. The reduction of the rabbit population through myxomatosis hit the fox population quite badly for a while, but they soon adapted to the problem, feeding on rats in place of rabbits and accepting more vegetable matter in their diets than they had previously. It is estimated that the fox's diet is normally 20 per cent vegetable matter, even in good hunting country, but in the days immediately after myxomatosis, foxes haunted rubbish dumps and bakeries and still continued to thrive on a low-protein diet. One Chinese restaurant in Birmingham actually had foxes nesting under an outhouse and living almost exclusively on the waste from the pig-bins outside the restaurant.

Town foxes are extremely common today, whereas twenty years ago a fox in the centre of a city merited a letter to *The Times*. Myxomatosis and the obliteration of the rabbit population has altered their ecology greatly. City refuse dumps now harbour more foxes than most country districts, and though their pelts are rarely in prime, because of the ravages of mange mite, the skin of a city fox is still marketable. The presence of rats as much as waste food probably lures the foxes to these dumps. At one time I hunted foxes in Birmingham and took a fair haul in the most unlikely districts. City foxes are usually far more nocturnal than their country cousins, since the daytime bustle of a city would naturally be fairly terrifying to any wild animal.

Foxes normally mate early in the year, and the courtship is a particularly noisy one, the sounds ranging from high-pitched screams to staccato barks. After mating, the female normally excavates a rabbit earth, and though the male usually digs in near by, cohabitation virtually ceases after the vixen nears parturition. The gestation period is approximately fifty-four to fifty-six days, and the cubs are born blue-black to chocolate-brown in colour. Since the fox, unlike the badger, does not gather bedding, the cubs are born on the bare floor of the earth, and thus are thickly furred as insulation against the cold. Females invariably hunt for themselves, and there is some debate over whether or not the dog fox takes any part in the rearing of the litter.

Contrary to the popular idea, the fox rarely lives below ground the whole year round, preferring to spend the late spring and summer in corn, bracken or kale. Possibly temperature directly influences this choice of habitat, but I am inclined to believe the old country notion that foxes leave the earths in summer because of the increase in the breeding rate of the mange mite (brought about by the warm weather), for summer-caught foxes are rarely badly infected with mange. It should also be said that the mange mite sees off more foxes in Great Britain than all hunts and lurchers put together.

The cutting of the corn and the reduction of the cover through autumnal die-off sees the fox back in its earth, and for a while cubs seem to congregate in the main earth, though this is also a time of aggression which, in various other beasts, sees the establishment of an order of peck or dominance. In foxes, however, the fighting merely ensures that the litter will spread out over a wider area. This is the period when pelts become prime and free from moult marks (which show up blue on a dried pelt). A few months later on will find the pelts of males damaged by sexually motivated or territorial battles. This is therefore the time to take a pelt if one is to get the best price for it.

Taking a pelt is one thing, catching the fox perhaps another. Basically, there are two methods of taking fox by the use of a lurcher. The first is to pin him in the beam of a lamp, for it is nearly

First fox – a 14 lb vixen.

impossible (except by the wildest chance) to catch one unaware in the daytime. The second method is to find the fox at home, bolt him with terriers and take him with a lurcher.

The first task, however, is to generate in the dog an unnatural antipathy to the foxes, and all canine antipathy to foxes is decidedly unnatural. A poor-grade pelt should be used to tease the dog, bringing it to a state of frenzy at the appearance of the pelt. Next the carcass of a fox should be placed before the dog, and he should be allowed to worry the cadaver. Some dogs become so frenzied in the worrying of a fox that they will literally ravage a carcass to pieces. Dogs of this disposition are undoubtedly in the right frame of mind to take a fox. If it is at all possible to allow the dog to see, or join in, a course at a fox, it is good policy to do so, though few pelt hunters will allow the tyro dog a chance to come in on a kill, rag the body and ruin the pelt. On the other hand, it is money invested to allow the younger dog a chance to be in at the kill.

With the dog in the right frame of mind, it is now time to make a bid for a fox. Lamping foxes is usually reasonably easy, provided the area chosen is unlamped and the foxes 'green' to the ways of lampers. Usually foxes are quite fascinated by the lamp and the lamper.

A bonanza haul of foxes, bolted by terriers, coursed by lurchers.

During a rabbit hunt, all the lamper needs to do is to swing the lamp around the field behind him to catch the large, luminous, moon-shaped eyes of a fox viewing the whole procedure with curiosity – and curiosity can do wonders for a fox, as it did for the cat. Unlike a rabbit, whose ruby eyes will often guide a lamper to the prey, the fox soon realizes that he is about to become a pelt and turns his eyes out of the beam, an action that makes him very difficult to see. The lurcher must now make do with running a shadowy shape. Once the lurcher has closed with his prey, the lamper should move in quickly to dispatch the fox, as painlessly and rapidly as possible. Not only is this humane, it is also excellent common sense. A fox fighting for its very life will put up a grim show and wound a lurcher quite badly before the finish. This is fine if one wants to see a duel to the death (if a little macabre, perhaps), but false economy if one wishes to hunt more than one fox a night. The fox, weighing only a little more than a large hare, is fairly easily finished by a large and hard dog, but the pelt hunter should help his dog whenever possible. Furthermore, a pelt from a fox that has literally slugged it out with a lurcher is apt to be

141

damaged, and therefore will fail to fetch a good price. Above all, it is brutal and wantonly cruel to allow a prolonged battle, and such behaviour brings discredit to the field sports that are already taking a bit of a beating from the anti-bloodsport faction. Tales of long and savage battles only serve to inflame society against the sport of coursing, and who can blame society for wanting to prevent further savagery.

Various methods may be used to get a fox to a suitable position to lamp, and the best of them is known as 'salting'. This involves the spreading of putrid offal, chicken bowels, paunch and so forth in a field or on waste ground where one intends to lamp, and then running and killing any fox keen enough for the easy life of scavenging. If the lamper waits downwind of the nauseous mess, then he will have an excellent chance of catching an unwary fox feeding. Foxes find even putrid offal quite acceptable, and some eight years ago I in fact grew potatoes on really putrid offal and found my crop ruined by foxes digging up the meat, even after the flesh was five or six months old and in a state of ripeness that would have deterred a hyena. Foxes seem totally immune to the ptomaine poisoning that must for most beasts inevitably follow such a meal. It also has to be remembered that dogs bitten by foxes that have fed on such filfth develop festering wounds unless they are treated promptly. A waste meat pile will draw foxes for miles. During 1977 I found four feeding on waste chicken guts that I had scattered and 'salted' near my house. Even an inept lurcher would have found little difficulty in making a kill in these conditions.

It is also possible to bring foxes into the range of the lamp by making a sucking noise. The sound is said to resemble the cry of a stricken rabbit, and it can be used to bring ferrets out of rabbit warrens. I'm rather doubtful as to whether the fox really thinks the cry is being emitted by a stricken rabbit, but most will move in to investigate the strange cry, and, as I've said, curiosity is often the undoing of any predator. Rabbits killed during lamping, or better still, returned to hand alive and squealing, certainly attract foxes in to investigate the prospect of an easy meal. In the autumn of 1977, Graham Welstead, founder of the Ferret Club of Great Britain, was lamping rabbits with me on the Dyatt estate with a very soft-mouthed lurcher who had never been entered to fox. The dog took a few rabbits that evening, and retrieved each one to hand alive and unhurt. During one run he brought back a particularly noisy rabbit, and a young vixen ran within four feet of the dog to investigate the sound. My lurcher promptly dropped his rabbit and pursued the fox, finally pinning it against some pig wire, where it crouched, spitting and snarling at him like an enraged tomcat. The dog was mystified, but, as I have stated, no natural antipathy exists between dog and fox and this lurcher had never been entered to fox. After a few moments, he forsook his fox and ran back to his rabbit which had squatted in fear. He then retrieved his rabbit to hand, totally unabashed by his failure against the vixen.

Another method of taking foxes, especially popular in the North, is to bolt the foxes with terriers and course them with a lurcher. This requires a fair piece of teamwork if the sport is to be conducted properly. To begin with, the lurcher should be made to stand to one side of the earth, preferably between the earth and a nearby hedge, through which a fox is certain to run as soon as he bolts. After a while the lurcher becomes accustomed to working with a terrier, and even tracks the subterranean battle by ear, stationing itself outside the most likely bolthole with a cat-like stealth. Hardwick of Blaengarw in South Wales was an ace at this method, and he had numerous superbly trained lurchers, all as steady as rocks during the underground struggle 'twixt dog and fox, but all able to anticipate the hole through which the fox would bolt. Hardwick's dogs were invariably collie crosses, and he had trained them to a high standard of obedience – a necessary quality when working foxes bolted by terriers.

Taking foxes with a lurcher is an extremely efficient method of fox control. Too efficient, perhaps, and foxes in fact need some protection from lurchermen. The pelts of breeding animals are practically useless, and to kill a vixen suckling cubs is really killing the goose that lays the golden eggs. A litter of foxes can yield pelts worth as much as £90, though it must be stressed that not all cubs make adult life, for many become casualties as a consequence of snares, dogs and road traffic. I have yet to travel the M5 without observing at least one fox lying dead on the motorway, crushed by passing cars. Overhunting will quickly kill off all foxes, and the lurcherman would do well to observe what is a basic rule for fox hunting all over the country. No hunt (except the Fell packs sometimes) hunts foxes when they are breeding.

Deer

Here, indeed, is a delicate subject, and before this book is published, the law regarding the taking of deer may have changed. Pattinson, in his lurcher chapter of the book *Coursing*, states that only make-believe lurchers will take deer. I suggest he glances at the daily newspapers once in a while to find out the truth about his statement. Furthermore, the incredible atrocities portrayed in *Shooting Times*, namely, deer with vicera hanging from the abdominal cavity and fawns torn out of the uteri of hinds and does, should convince him of the error of his beliefs. Deer have become the number-one animal target for poachers, and the publicity given to the subject has aroused a great deal of public indignation, particularly in towns where people see the deer as an ever-young Walt Disney creation, a Bambi-type of beast. Sentimentality aside, the fact is that Britain is becoming denuded of its deer population through poachers. Cannock Chase, one of the last sanctuaries of the fallow deer, is now a real stamping ground for the poacher, and unless something is done quickly to stop deer poaching and the resultant mangling of these animals, the field-sport fraternity of Britain may shortly rue the day when the average poacher turned his attention from rabbits to deer. Hunting deer with dogs which hamstring, cripple and disembowel deer is likely to be the lever the anti-bloodsport societies need to topple the British Field Sports Society.

Regarding deer, there are several varieties still to be found in Britain, ranging from the tiny water deer to the red deer. Most species are quaint, Oriental imports brought into Britain during Victorian times by colonial types who rather regretted having to return from the Orient and brought in these odd little creatures as memorabilia of the Far East. The rare Père David's deer was imported from the deer parks of China, where it was carefully guarded to prevent the species becoming extinct, it having died out in the wild almost 3,000 years ago. Even this deer has been poached, though its flesh is reputed to have a strong musky taste. During the mid 1970s, a deer poacher killed 180 sundry deer, including a few Père David, and received for his crimes a total of six months for this and other convictions for burglary. He did well, really, when one considers that the deer he killed were valued by prosecuting counsel at £12,000. Even assuming that our poacher failed to get a good price for the venison (and most poachers are woefully robbed by the receivers, who are aware that their clients are unlikely to complain about any lack of fairness), then £20,000 a year for poaching makes the prison sentence seem a trivial setback for him to say the least. The deer preservation societies were left smarting after such an insult to their work, I am sure.

It is most unlikely that any deer hunter will be able to obtain legal permission to course deer, yet nearly every advertisement for lurchers in *Exchange and Mart* lists deer among the quarry taken by their dogs or offspring. Deer are usually poached by lamping and approaching the bewildered beast with lurcher on the slip. At the very last moment, the lurcher is slipped and will catch hold wherever it can on the deer's body. Most poachers will boast that their dogs invariably go for a throat hold, and that little cruelty is involved in the taking of quarry. In practice, the unerring throat bite is rarely put in, for in the rough and tumble of a lamped deer course, most dogs will catch hold of any portion of the deer they can reach, and hang on. The legendary throat hold is invariably offered as a defence by the poacher convicted of deer poaching, his offence made more serious by a simultaneous prosecution by the RSPCA for wanton cruelty to the deer.

It is lunacy to suggest that no or even minimal cruelty is involved when two lurchers pull down a fallow or red deer, and anyone foolish

145

enough to believe that the death of the deer is instantaneous in these circumstances should actually witness such a hunt. As a rule, the RSPCA push their cruelty cases quite hard, and it is this estimable society that badgers magistrates, still besotted by the romanticism associated with poaching, into handing down fines of £2,000 to deer poachers. Magistrates are incurable romantics, it seems, and regard every villain in search of deer as a type of latter-day Robin Hood. It is pleasing to see that the RSPCA are considerably more realistic about the brutality involved in deer poaching.

For the purpose of this section, however, we must assume that the hunter is one of those rare creatures: a man who has permission to hunt deer with sight hounds. It is difficult to get, this permission, and even difficult to say with one's tongue in one's cheek. But details of the British deer are now required.

The Red Deer

This is the largest of the British deer, and also the least poached. Not only does its size offer opposition to the average lurcher, or even super-lurcher, but its environment makes poaching with lurchers somewhat difficult. Originally it was a forest dweller, browsing rather than grazing, but man, with his encroaching cities and persistent hunting, has pushed this exquisite creature to the remoter moors of Dartmoor, Exmoor and, of course, the Scottish Highlands. This is the deer which Landseer depicted in his *Monarch of the Glen* painting, whose draughtsmanship is not diminished by the monotonous obsession Edwardian England seemed to have with this animal portrait. In size, the red deer measures up to 54 inches at the shoulder, and some stags weigh up to 15 and 16 stone. It is likely that moorland grazing does not wholly suit this forest dweller, for the antlers of modern deer have grown considerably smaller than antlers taken during medieval times.

The gestation period of the hinds is roughly nine months, and calving occurs in May or June. Within hours of the birth, the calves can run quite well – so well, in fact, that a man would be hard pressed to take one. In spite of this independence, the calf stays with its dam until it is ten months old. The male becomes sexually mature at about four years old, though the famous royal sets of antlers are not usually achieved until the sixth year.

Antlers, while splendid objects, serve very little purpose, it appears. True, they can help to down an attacking dog. Henry Williamson's Deadlock, the anti-hero hound of the book, *Tarka the Otter*, had been cleaved, or disembowelled, by deer, but in the art of

146

fighting the deer's own kind, antlers are inclined to be a bit of a dis-
advantage. Hummels, or antlerless stags (no less virile for their lack
of status symbols), invariably defeat antlered stags in the fight for
hinds. It now seems likely that antlers serve only to allow heat to
radiate from the body.

As for the taking of red deer with lurchers, all that can be said is
that it is possible for a pair of well-trained dogs to hold a red deer, but
the carnage is going to be quite frightful. They are poached rarely
because of this, coupled, of course, with the fact that they are now
moorland dwellers and therefore difficult to approach, which makes
them difficult quarry. A battle between a red deer and two or more
lurchers is fairly sickening, since the deer's size makes it difficult to
pull down for the poacher to dispatch. It must be fully understood
that even a team of lurchers will need considerable help in finishing
an adult red stag, and here I am afraid we come to the nasty bit. Since
the time when the Forest Laws were being passed, man has hunted
deer with hounds of the scent-hound variety, hounds similar to large
and powerful foxhounds. These dogs would bring the stag to bay, and
a member of the hunt would creep behind the deer and quickly and
deftly cut its throat. It is virtually a conjuror's trick, and it needs
great skill and training to perfect. Mention is made of these men by
Gaston Phoebus and other medieval writers, who eulogized on the
skill of this hunt servant.

It is extremely unlikely that any modern deer poacher, or amateur
deer hunter, would have such skills, so the dispatching of a red
invariably degenerates into a sickening stabbing match, with the
poacher stabbing hither and thither at the wounded and threshing
stag. It is a gory, messy and horribly inhuman act to watch, and
decidedly to be frowned on by any sane and reasonable person. Sometimes so many wounds are made on the deer that the carcass is
unsaleable, even to the seediest dealer in game. Altogether, the taking
of red deer with lurchers is an extremely nasty form of poaching, and
one that magistrates should be made to watch before passing the
ridiculously lenient sentences that are all too common in the courts.

The Fallow Deer

This is the deer that is suffering most from the present spate of deer
poaching. In spite of its picturesque and typically English look, the
fallow deer is not a native of Britain, though the name 'fallow' is derived
from the Anglo-Saxon *fealwe*, meaning 'greyish-brown'. Men introduced this beast to Britain from the Mediterranean lands, although

147

fossil remains seem to suggest that, prior to the last Ice Age, it was formerly common in Britain. The Romans are credited with its re-introduction, though this, again, is largely conjecture and backed by no scientific facts.

The fallow was regarded as Royal Quarry, and the forests into which they were turned became Royal Forests, or were enclosed to make parks. Savage punishments protected the deer from harassment by the common man, and perhaps this was a good thing, or else the deer would not have survived. Numerous mentions are made of these punishments in folk-songs. In addition to the ubiquitous ballads about Robin Hood, the song 'Geordie' gives an indication that the punishment for deer poaching was still hanging, even in the late seventeenth century. This, too, is the deer which Will Shakespeare was caught poaching, if there is any truth in that story. By looking at its habits and structure, however, we can easily see why this deer should be so popular with the poaching fraternity.

The fallow deer kept in enclosed parks were literally sitting-ducks for the poacher, for, large as the parks were, they offered no protection against a poacher equipped with running dogs and guile. It is also worth noting that the fallow deer has a very high 'dress out' weight, so there is little that is not edible in the carcass, and hence the deer fetches a high price – very high when one considers the ease with which it can be taken.

Fallow deer feed at dawn or dusk, and old bucks are strictly nocturnal. On Royal Forests such as Cannock Chase, Epping Forest or the New Forest, an early-morning drive in a car will usually find small parties of deer feeding by the roadside, browsing on grasses and moss. Gipsy folk are said to eat the partly digested moss found in the stomach of deer, which is reputed to taste like spinach, but I can find no one who has actually tried this nauseous-sounding delicacy. Certainly such a dish would be hard to digest, as deer rarely feed exclusively on mosses, preferring to browse on twigs and branches as much as on other herbage.

The rut, or mating, occurs in October, when each fallow buck behaves wildly, marking out its own territory with display and musk. Fights between rivals rarely become very serious, for as soon as supremacy is settled, the loser is more than prepared to slink away. Fawns are born in May or June, and when startled will freeze to escape detection, their dappled brown blending well with the undergrowth of the forest. Normally the doe will not rejoin the herd until the fawn is able to run with the herd, and some stay with their dams for as long as two years. By the time the deer is two years of age, the bucks are approaching nearly three feet at the shoulder and have a dazzling burst of speed. Truly the fallow deer is a fascinating animal, and one well worth maintaining in our crowded land.

Hunting permission to take these deer with sight hounds or lurchers is rarely, if ever, granted, and most fallow deer taken by lurchers are poached. It is true that some feral deer may be culled on farms or private forests where they have become a nuisance, and these are sometimes taken legally with lurchers or greyhounds. In any circumstances, however, it is a messy and nasty process. As the fallow deer is smaller than the red by a good 18 inches, it can rarely overmatch a pair of lurchers. It is actually very difficult to enter a lurcher to deer, particularly those that are well trained and broken to sheep. Normally these dogs need a great deal of encouragement and example from another dog before they will engage so large a quarry. Furthermore, the dogs used to take deer need to see deer pulled over before they become really proficient at the technique. Again, many hunters boast neck dogs, or dogs that will fly at the throat of the retreating deer. Few dogs have this precision, as the mangled carcasses that appear after poaching onslaughts in Epping Forest have shown. Like the red, the fallow is too large for a dog to kill quickly, and the worrying of one to death is a singularly unpleasant spectacle. Hunters who have taken these deer usually dispatch them quickly by cutting the throats or breaking the necks of the fawns. It is noteworthy that poachers who take these deer will usually get rid of their knives as soon as they are approached, as the possession of arms, in the form of knives, usually ensures a substantial increase in the punishments issued by magistrates. Most fallow deer are taken by lamping on a dark and gusty night.

The Roe Deer

The roe deer is a lot more widespread than most people imagine. Animals are perverse creatures, and should man seek to protect them they promptly become extinct. Likewise, if a beast is ignored, it invariably prospers. Thus, until recently, the roe deer was actually on the increase, though its shy nature and nocturnal habits make it a difficult subject to study.

This deer is smaller than the fallow, and it is a very large buck which reaches 70 pounds in weight, most measuring only about 2 feet 6 inches at the shoulder. Does are smaller, most weighing under 45 pounds in weight, and in some districts quite diminutive adults are found, the loss in size probably being caused by inbreeding. No animal has the stealth and bushcraft of a roe deer, and their ability to move noiselessly through woodlands has to be seen to be believed. They literally blend into cover and rarely cause a twig to crack as they move through quite thick undergrowth. This deer is also quite a good swimmer, and will readily take to water to evade the hunter or to reach new feeding grounds.

Mating involves a curious ceremony, with the buck chasing the doe around a bush or tree in a tight circle or figure-of-eight. Once the doe is sexually aroused, the buck will mate her within the circle – or roe rings, as countrymen call them. Mating normally occurs in July or August, though implantation of the embryo is delayed and takes place in December. In the following May, the doe will usually produce one or two kids (the young of the roe deer being called 'kids' rather than 'fawns'). These kids are usually small and helpless, and many apparently fall prey to foxes. Anyone wishing to hunt these deer, either by stalking and shooting or else by killing them with dogs, would do well to read the researches of Richard Prior on the habits of the roe deer. It was, in fact, Prior's researches, which are quite estimable pieces of scientific workmanship, that gave the Forestry Commission a clear understanding of the destructive ways of the roe bucks and proved that a well-culled herd did negligible damage to forestry. An over-bucked herd, on the other hand, is extremely destructive since the celibate bucks take out their spleen and excess energy on bushes and trees. The roe buck is, in fact, quite an aggressive beast, and the taking of a roe buck fawn as a pet is sheer lunacy. In spite of their appealing looks, roe bucks kept in captivity usually become highly savage towards their owners and will attack and frequently kill dogs and rush strangers on sight. It is also worth remembering that a 70-pound horned adversary should not be taken lightly. I know of several instances where dogs and people have been savagely mauled by a tame roe buck on the rampage.

This deer is often taken by dogs, and a good strong coursing dog has only a little trouble in taking and holding a roe. I say 'holding' with one reservation, for the hunter should be in on the kill quickly to prevent cruelty to the deer and damage to the dog, for the roe buck is quite a strong animal and threshes about considerably when taken. Again, this deer falls victim to the callous brutality of the deer poacher, though its very nature makes it difficult quarry to lamp successfully. It is frequently taken by lurchers in the North of England where the roe deer seems relatively common.

Before closing this chapter, a word of advice is necessary. Dogs run at deer regularly tend to become unsure as to whether or not sheep are legitimate quarry, and it often becomes difficult to course the dog at hares in sheep country where hares will use feeding flocks as they would cover. Sheep often fall victim to the dogs of deer hunters, though most deer poachers I have met frequently admit to not being averse to adding a sheep to the night's bag. All of this is hardly conducive to the furtherance of field sports, and it certainly gets lurchermen a bad name. Only recently, cases of cattle stealing by using dogs to bring down half-grown calves have hit the headlines. Truly, these lunatic lurcher-men are doing the sporting world a great deal of harm.

If a lurcherman has a dog that is keen on taking deer, he would do well to shut up about it. Not only are the police and RSPCA more than interested in the activities of such dogs, but mention of deer dogs will attract an amazing collection of highly undesirable people to his house. Strange people resembling characters out of a scene by Hieronymus Bosch will haunt the house of the owner of such a dog, making offers for the purchase of his deer-killing lurcher. The lurcherman with a yen to take deer should realize that the police soon look on him in the same light as they do the grotesque oddities frequenting his house in the hope of buying his dog. The simple fact is that deer are best left alone by lurchermen.

11 *The Breeding of Lurchers*

Quite simply, lurchers are bred by three distinct types of mating:

(1) Mating pure-bred sight hounds with pure-bred non-sight hounds (or different sight hound types).
(2) The mating of a lurcher to a greyhound, or similar sight hound.
(3) The mating of a lurcher to a lurcher.

We must now consider these matings so as to assess the relative merits in breeding in these ways.

First-Cross Matings

In spite of the spate of advertisements stating that puppies for sale are first cross, this type of mating is very, very uncommon. Such matings are usually conducted by men who seek to create an ideal lurcher, having grown a little discontented with the lurchers they have owned. It is rather a far-sighted plan which usually involves a fair degree of wastage coupled with considerable financial outlay. First, the would-be lurcher breeder must acquire either a greyhound bitch or the services of a greyhound dog. Next he must acquire the other breed (or services of a sire of the other breed). It is unlikely that the dogs used in this mating will have value in coursing, so after the breeder has acquired the puppy he wants he is left with the dam of the puppies (and possibly the sire), and must either harden his heart and get rid of her, or at least put her out to pasture. Admittedly, a greyhound bitch can usually be obtained for next to nothing, or as being simply 'free to a good home', but the breeding of such a litter involves extra housing and the feeding of a pensioned-off bitch should she be kept.

Few lurchermen have the facilities for a breeding programme of this kind, so first crosses are rarely attempted, no matter what the avertisements say. Quite a few commercial breeders do, however, use the method to produce puppies – now more than ever, for the lurcher falls a close second to the Jack Russell terrier as the most fashionable breed at the time of writing. It is, in fact, commercially extremely viable to breed lurchers by this method, as the non-sight-hound sire need not be a show specimen (and can therefore be obtained quite cheaply), and the greyhound bitches can be had for the begging. Lurchermen usually fight shy of such commercial breeders, as the breeder is rarely a coursing man and is motivated to breed lurchers for cash consideration. I assure the reader that, provided the puppies are well reared and the vendor is a *bona fide* breeder, the puppies will be none the worse for their owner's mercenary motive. In fact, most puppies bred by commercial breeders are usually better reared than puppies produced by back-yard breeders with little or no knowledge of the whelping of a bitch and the rearing of puppies. At one time Nuttall of Clitheroe bred some first-class coursing dogs by mating his pure-bred deerhound stud to greyhound bitches. Only recently, I noticed that a commercial breeder in Herne Bay was selling collie/greyhound first-cross hybrids and also collie/saluki crosses. There is one word of advice for the would-be purchaser, however. Many breeders are on the level about their dogs, but there is a number who are suspect, and who quite simply buy mongrel lurcher puppies to sell as collie/greyhound, Bedlington/greyhound and so on hybrids. The would-be buyer needs to be careful about his purchaser and to avoid the doubtful breeder like the plague.

Legitimate breeders are quite thin on the ground, whereas dealers abound. The puppies obtained from such dealers could be extremely useful despite their dubious pedigrees, and, after all, what's in a name? But the constant stream of puppies passing through a dealer's hands are bound to introduce disease into his premises sooner or later. Few of these dealers have kennels that would pass muster for a breeder's licence, and their premises are usually havens for mange, skin parasites and, worse still, leptospirosis or, dread of dreads, distemper. Furthermore, few of these dealers have scruples enough to stop peddling their wares when disease does hit their dogs. Frankly, lurcher dealers are best avoided, not because of their dishonesty, though many simply buy cheap and sell dear, but because of the danger of buying an infected puppy from them. *Caveat emptor*, 'Let the buyer beware', should always be the motto of the would-be lurcher purchaser.

Lurcher to Greyhound Matings

This is quite a common way of obtaining lurchers, particularly if the breeder has a useful but heavy-built lurcher bitch and the use of a good greyound stud. The reasons for the cross are many. First, the addition of greyhound blood to the miscellaneous hotch-potch of breeds that most lurchers consist of will usually have a levelling effect on the litter, with little or no wastage. Secondly, the crossing of a nondescript lurcher with a greyhound produces an exceptionally fast dog. And lastly, but not least, the addition of further greyhound blood to a shapeless and unattractive lurcher produces a very good-looking animal – a point to consider when the country is becoming pro-lurcher and it is fashionable to own this former pariah of the canine world. The number of lurchers who have never so much as seen a rabbit or a hare must be very great at the time of writing. This statement is not meant to belittle those who do not work their lurchers, and who prefer to show them and keep them as companion dogs; and if all the lurchers seen at shows caught and killed game, the country would be denuded of life in no time. Dogs with a high proportion of greyhound blood will win very well at shows.

It would be wise to mention that the addition of greyhound blood to an already finely built strain of lurcher does little to help it further. Not only will the puppies from such a mating be lacking in stamina, but the addition of further greyhound blood does little to improve the hunting instinct, the nose or, above all, the intelligence of the lurcher. Constant addition of greyhound blood will in time produce a dog that is nearly pure greyhound, and this is not really wanted. Before the lurcher breeder produces a litter, he should give thought to the qualities he wants in the end product. If he requires a very trainable dog, too much greyhound has a decidedly deleterious effect on the tractability of the puppies.

This is, perhaps, the moment to mention the problems of breeding from greyhounds, and there are many.

The Problems

First, it is assumed that the greyhounds one is using to breed lurchers are track rejects and veteran animals. Assume, therefore, that one wishes to mate one's lurcher bitch to a greyhound dog and the chance of obtaining a retired greyhound dog comes one's way. Quite simply, many have little or no idea of how to mate. They have been kept solely for racing, and therefore any interest in bitches has been discouraged. By the age of four or five, a greyhound may be fertile enough but totally lacking in the notion of how to mate a bitch. Most make a half-hearted attempt at stud work, and many simply regard an in-season bitch with utter bewilderment, greeting her with tail-wagging *bonhomie* and little else besides. It is often quite impossible to get such a dog to mate an in-season bitch.

Let us assume, therefore, that one wishes to resuscitate one's lurcher strain by mating a lurcher dog to a greyhound bitch. The bitch is easily obtainable, more easily so than a dog, in fact, for greyhound bitches are not raced during the months preceding and following a season. As soon as he has one which has aged just a little, the 'flapping track' greyhound man will be eager to find a home for his ward. A greyhound bitch is thus obtained, and one is not out of the wood yet. Many greyhound bitches come in season twice a year, as do other breeds, but many more are extremely erratic in coming in season. Obviously greyhound-racing men prefer a bitch who comes in season infrequently, as she will be off the track for a far shorter period of time. Therefore 'once a year' season bitches are numerous, and the lurcher breeder may find he has to wait several months before he can mate his lurcher dog to a greyhound bitch. Here, again, the would-be lurcher breeder's problems are not at an end. Many greyhound bitches are extremely difficult to mate. Not only do they have extremely erratic seasons, lasting for nearly a month in some cases (during which time they are fertile for only a few days), but many have vaginas that are very small indeed, and it takes a trained stud dog to penetrate and tie with such an animal.

Most professional greyhound breeders employ full-time stud grooms to ensure that greyhounds couple, and many of these stud grooms are extremely skilful at their job. They often use amazing methods to get difficult bitches to mate, and some even resort to surgery to ensure that the dog is able to penetrate the bitch and tie with her. Few lurcher breeders have such skills, and back-yard lurcher breeders would do well to lay out some money on a bitch that is known to be fertile and easy to mate. As a ray of hope to illuminate the gloom created by the last few paragraphs, it must be stated that, once mated, few greyhound bitches have trouble in whelping, but we shall deal with the problems of parturition later in the chapter.

Lurcher x Lurcher Matings

This is undoubtedly the most common and popular way of producing lurchers, and the reasons for the popularity are obvious once we examine the subject. First, it is clearly the best method from the point of view of economy, for one is not buying a useless animal (useless from the point of view of hunting, that is) like a greyhound, but merely breeding from a tried and tested bitch that has earned her keep before breeding and will possibly earn her keep later. Secondly, stud dogs are easy to obtain. While most lurcher breeders do not actually encourage their dogs to display an interest in bitches, few try hard to discourage it. Furthermore, the dog has usually been socialized by intimate contact with human beings and is therefore reasonably certain to welcome his owner's assistance when he mates a bitch. Many lurcher dogs are also simply allowed to run free and to learn their sex education in the street with cur bitches.

It is, indeed, a fact that such a life does actually assist the prowess of a stud dog. Gipsies have a saying that the most useful greyhound studs are those which have been left to run the streets. Furthermore, whereas the greyhound trainer will probably have some qualms about allowing a top-class dog to mate a lurcher bitch (foolishly, since it doesn't harm the dog), few lurchermen will deny their dogs a chance to serve a bitch, particularly if the mating will produce a fee, or a very saleable puppy in lieu of fee. These facts will enable the reader to realize why lurcher x lurcher matings are very common indeed. Now for the disadvantages.

Few lurchers are what the advertisement says they are. Most change hands a few times before breeding, and pedigrees are lost in the process. Thus any dog displaying a slightly rough coat is immediately, for the sake of convenience, labelled a deerhound/greyhound, and the most unlikely dogs masquerade as collie/greyhounds. Most lurchers are at root simply a canine morass with a liberal, or not so liberal, dose of sight hound, and unless one is absolutely certain as to the pedigree of one's dog, the mating of two lurchers can produce some amazing progeny. Pattinson advises the mating of two similar types of lurcher, and while it can be said that some useful lurchers are produced by this mating, it should be added that some fairly horrible specimens are produced as well. This brings us to the question of why such monsters should appear in litters.

First, let us assume that one has a straight-cross collie/greyhound bred by a legitimate breeder, and that while the offspring is bright, fast and easily trainable, it is also a little nesh. Suppose, therefore, that one wishes to breed a more gutsy, gamer type of dog, and so you mate the bitch to a game Bedlington/greyhound hybrid, also legitimately bred. It is now necessary to illustrate the breeding process by letters, so we will call the Collie C, the Bedlington B and the Greyhound G. Before the reader goes further, it must be emphasized that genetics is a science, governed by mathematical laws, and not simply a mixing of genes like colours in a paint box. Now for the progeny of the cross.

C G x B G

This cross could produce:

$\frac{1}{4}$ nearly pure greyhound
$\frac{1}{2}$ mixture of Bedlington, collie and greyhound
$\frac{1}{4}$ mixture of collie and Bedlington, with little by way of greyhound being inherited.

Steve Jones' noted show champion lurcher – a useful coursing and show dog.

Take, therefore, another instance, Walsh, in his *Lurchers and Long Dogs*, mentions that many strains of collie/greyhounds will breed fairly true, but that even then the wastage is fairly great.

C G   x   C G

Could easily give you:

$\frac{1}{4}$ nearly pure greyhound
$\frac{1}{2}$ collie/greyhound types
$\frac{1}{4}$ nearly pure collie.

Now the lurcher breeder, or aspirant lurcher breeder, must envisage the odd miscellany of puppies that can result from mating two lurchers of doubtful origin, and it should be mentioned that the majority of lurchers seen at shows have twenty or thirty crosses in their ancestry. Thus, odd-looking animals will frequently be produced in lurcher litters when two lurchers of doubtful origin are mated. Dogs resembling mastiffs, Danes and collies crop up with regularity among such litters. Even so, as Pattinson comments, some cracking good ones appear in

157

them as well. Because of the capricious results, however, I would never buy dogs from a gipsy camp, as few of them are properly bred and very rarely is a mating supervised, most of the dogs being allowed to run the camp and mate willy-nilly. The tragedy is, of course, that lurchers take a long time to develop and change shape almost daily. Thus we have the situation where an outstanding-looking puppy may develop into a cloddy monster whereas a little brother sold as not the right type becomes a thing of breathtaking beauty. Some strains of lurcher, particularly those with a fair amount of sight-hound blood in them, breed relatively true to type, and it is rumoured that certain strains are already breeding as true to type as any Kennel Club registered breed. Pattinson advocates an occasional mating with greyhound to keep up the speed of the strain, and his words are wise.

The Mating Process

As for the actual mating, there is an opinion that it is unwise to breed from a bitch during her first season since this stunts her growth. Frankly, the idea is ludicrous and is certainly unsupported by scientific evidence. It is nevertheless unwise to breed from a first-season bitch, but for totally different reasons. Most bitches first come into season at between nine months and a year old. This is usually a critical time in training, the time when the first rays of commonsense are penetrating the foolishness of puppyhood. Thus, a bitch will be far better employed in going through an intensive training programme at this age than in being used for breeding. Again, it must be mentioned that season, or sexual maturity, is not always equated with mental maturity, and many bitches who produce puppies as a result of a mating during their first season are a little baffled over what to do with them. The bitch's maternal instinct may well be quite strong at this age, and the litter be reared well, but sometimes this is not the case, and the bitch may reject the litter totally, or scatter them around the shed; or, worse still, become so over-protective towards them that she keeps carrying them around the pen in her mouth – attractive to see, but very bruising for the puppy, and bruised puppies often die. Weighing up the pros and cons of first-season mating, it does not seem very sensible to mate a bitch so early in her career, though the whelping of such a bitch, whose pelvic bones are soft and pliable, is considerably easier than the whelping of a veteran animal.

There is yet another point to consider. At nine months old a lurcher is, to use a country expression, 'neither mickling nor muckling', and it is still in the lap of the gods (and the trainer) whether or not the bitch will become a useful animal, worthy of perpetuating the family. If it is one's wish merely to produce puppies for sale, then it might be advisable to breed from first-season bitches, and every season, for that matter, from then on. However, if it is one's wish to produce an outstanding lurcher puppy, it is wise to test the dam to the utmost before breeding from her, for no better proof of the pudding exists than the field of hunting. It is a wise man indeed who can say whether or not a nine-month-old bitch is likely to turn out to be a really good hunting animal.

At the other end of the scale, it is unwise to breed from a bitch that is senile, though a bitch just past her best as a coursing or racing animal is, at maybe five or six years old, usually quite suitable as a brood bitch. The hard and strenuous life of a lurcher does a great deal to keep the body in tone, and many lurchers will breed for many years after retirement from the coursing field. Ten- or eleven-year-old bitches will frequently produce healthy litters, though breeding from a ten-year-old bitch for the first time is likely to bring some problems. Provided the bitch is sound and healthy, however, then she can be used to breed puppies. Greyhounds and greyhound types of dog are physically the most perfect of the canine world, so little deformity of the pelvis or womb is encountered as a rule, and the type is usually free from the exaggeration which the show breeder has bred into most breeds – exaggerations that make natural whelping damn nigh imposs-ible in some animals. Few problems are encountered when whelping a litter of lurchers.

In dealing with the actual process of mating, we must frankly acknowledge that the breeding of dogs is surrounded with old wives' tales, most of which are harmlessly unscientific, while a few are downright dangerous. It is perhaps fortunate that lurchers whelp so easily, for the worst perpetrators of old wives' tales are lurcher breeders themselves.

A bitch will usually come into season at roughly nine months old. 'Usually', however, does not apply to a greyhound type of breed, which must be the most irregular of all breeds in its oestrus cycle. I have known greyhounds and other sight hounds, even lurchers, not come into season until their third year, possibly because God, in his wisdom, has decreed that the dogs were not physically or emotionally ready to breed until that time. Once a bitch comes into season, however, the breeding cycle becomes fairly regular and she will come into season at six-monthly or yearly cycles from the date of the first season.

Season commences with the tissue just above the vagina growing turgid, and this is followed by a swelling of the vagina itself and a menstrual discharge. Normally, when a bitch is passing this bloody fluid, she will attract the attention of a male, particularly a stud of some experience, but she will resent any attempted act of mating as yet, even going so far as to snap at the dog. Her actions, however, will not be as serious as they would have been had a dog tried to mate her half-way between her seasons. On the twelfth day although this is by no means precise for all bitches) the bloody discharge will have ceased and the vagina be very swollen. This is commonly the time when a bitch will accept the attentions of a dog. A surer test is for the owner to pass his hands down the flanks of a bitch, imitating the pressure of a mating dog, and if she is ready for mating, she will turn her tail aside and push her vagina towards him. At this period in their season bitches are usually very fertile, and a mating at this time will be most likely to produce puppies.

A dog will be most interested in a bitch in this condition, and after considerable licking and sex play (which should always be allowed), he will endeavour to mount her. The mating action of all canines is not only incongruous, but is biologically baffling, for it leaves both dog and bitch in a highly vulnerable condition. A few breed books give explanations for the act, but so far no convincing reason has been offered as to why dogs mate in the manner they do, and it would be madness for me to advance a theory to explain the act. At all events, the dog pushes his penis into the vagina and thrusts deeply inside the bitch, his back legs actually leaving the ground during the act of penetration. Once the dog has completely penetrated the bitch's vagina, the end of his penis becomes distended, which often causes the bitch considerable pain. She will pull away, screaming, and may well try to savage the dog, even going so far as to roll on the ground to get away from him. She is prevented from doing this by the fact that the penis inside her becomes swollen until it is far larger than the vagina. The dog will, at this point, drop his front legs and shift his body position until he is standing back to back with the bitch. After a few moments of this part of the mating, the bitch will usually grow very calm.

This position, known as a 'tie' to dog breeders, is fairly essential to the mating. While some bitches will conceive without the tie, most will not. Frankly, I would never take or give a stud fee for a bitch who has had a dog penetrate her unless they have tied. Usually such matings are fruitless. The length of the time the pair remain attached is very variable, ranging between about twenty minutes and two hours. Stories of Great Danes and mastiffs remaining tied for frightening lengths of time are legion but, again, uninvestigated. After mating, the dog will withdraw his penis, usually still very swollen, and will pass tiny jets of semen in the act of withdrawal. Some semen also runs from the bitch.

Once, when mating a greyhound stud I owned to a lurcher bitch that was brought to him for mating, the owner of the bitch noticed the semen running from the animal and promptly grabbed the bitch and held her head-downwards, legs in the air, to prevent the loss of semen. I stood for a matter of a minute or two watching him, absolutely fascinated by the act, while he started to explain that unless he prevented the loss of semen the bitch could not possibly conceive. Wild dogs also mate as tame dogs, and I doubt if they stand on their heads after mating to prevent semen loss. It is, of course, totally superfluous to perform such a circus trick. Only excess semen is lost, and the dog will have passed enough fluid to guarantee conception.

During the mating act the couple are best held, however, for the convulsions of the bitch can easily rupture a dog and stories of dogs dying after such matings are not all that uncommon. People who advocate natural matings, allowing the dog to be dragged hither and thither by the screaming, snapping bitch, would find their dog very reluctant to mate after a few such sessions. A trained stud dog – trained by practice, that is – will sometimes decline to mount a bitch who is not being held. Once the initial shock of being mated has somewhat abated, the bitch will not need to be restrained as forcibly as she was at the start of the mating.

One mating at the correct time in the season will usually suffice, but, to ensure conception, several services are necessary. A bitch should be mated as often as possible during her season – once a day is not too much. This ensures, first, that the bitch has every chance of conceiving, and secondly, that the dog is producing fresh sperm at every mating. Tests have shown that a dog mated very infrequently will produce a great number of dead sperm during ejaculation. It is a true saying that a dog that is overused is more fertile than a dog that is underused. Moreover, frequent matings make a dog far more suitable for stud work than a dog that has had few bitches. If the dog is young and healthy, he can be used daily, and, in fact, every day of his adult life, without a great deal of harm. Allow him to be hurt during a mating, however, and the dog will take several weeks to forget the experience.

The Care of the Bitch in Pregnancy

Let us assume the bitch has been mated numerous times during her season, and that conception is more than likely. During season, bitches develop a great deal of fat over the ovaries and greyhounds are usually banned from racing in the months preceding and following a season. Lurchers can be hunted fairly actively, though not coursed to a state of exhaustion following the weeks of the mating. In fact, exercise has a beneficial effect since it tones up the walls of the uterus and allows the bitch to give birth to her puppies more easily. There is little danger of a bitch miscarrying, even after a violent course, but the dangers of heart failure after such treatment are very real. So keeping the bitch active, but not literally run off her feet, is the order of the day during this period.

By the time the bitch is three weeks pregnant her condition will begin to be obvious, even to the untrained observer. The loins will begin to fill out and the nipples start to become prominent. This is the time when most dog books advise the breeder to cram the bitch full of nourishing food on the grounds that she is eating for 'six plus instead of one'. It may seem logical to the dog breeder, who hopes for good, strong, healthy puppies, but it is, in fact, an action that is fraught with danger, and on examination it becomes obvious why. A wild canine bitch will eat less not more during her pregnancy, for her lack of ability to catch quarry in her bloated condition will see to that. Thus she must either suffer the loss of the foetuses or her body must make drastic changes.

There is evidence to suggest that the body, or at least the digestive tracts, do go through quite a few changes during pregnancy. First, the gut must make use of less food, so it becomes correspondingly more efficient, absorbing more protein from the food which passes through. At normal times, the dog's digestive system is rather wasteful, absorbing only a proportion of protein-rich substances. During pregnancy, the gut absorbs most of the protein ingested, and so excessive feeding during pregnancy will lead to extra food being absorbed, and this in turn will result in obesity in the bitch and over-large foetuses. Thus a flabby, overweight bitch will give birth to very large puppies which she may have considerable difficulty in passing. While it must be admitted that the lower condition of the wild canine bitch usually results in the loss of some of her puppies, it must be stressed that cramming a pregnant bitch with food is not only inadvisable but positively dangerous. Likewise, feeding a healthy bitch extra vitamins, and particularly mineral salts such as calcium lactate, can also be fairly hazardous. Food should be increased slightly during the last weeks of pregnancy, and this will allow the puppies to be born fit and well, but, again, the word 'slightly' does not mean to excess.

By the seventh week of pregnancy, the bitch will be filling out rapidly and some of the teats will be very prominent. The gestation of a normal bitch can be between fifty-eight and sixty-three days, the latter figure being correct in a dog of lurcher size, the former more likely in bitches of terrier size. At this point the bitch will seem a little anxious, and from the seventh week she will be constantly preparing a nest for her offsprings. She may pull together the bedding in her shed or constantly be nosing at piles of it in a corner, but she will become quite frantic during the period immediately preceding parturition. As she comes close to whelping, a bitch usually scratches frantically at her straw, even digging at the bare boards of her pen. This action is distressing only to the watcher. It is perfectly normal, and its absence is usually an indication that something is going wrong. A bitch who appears sluggish and lethargic at this time of pregnancy is probably toxaemic and in need of veterinary attention. The violent scratching action immediately prior to parturition is one of the good signs. Several bitches I have known have dug up the brick floors of their whelping sheds during this period.

Whelping and the Care of the Litter

The first signs that birth is imminent are the enlarging of the vagina to take the passage of the puppies and a slight straining of the muscles of the bitch's womb. The bitch will now begin to bear down, and a clear sac of slightly greenish membrane will emerge from the vagina. This bag is filled with watery fluid, pungent and slightly bitter to the taste, and should not be broken. The liquid within acts as a lubricant for the passage of the puppy. Should the bag burst, this lubricant will drain away and the subsequent dry delivery will be more difficult and certainly more painful for the bitch. Within a matter of an hour or so, further straining will begin and the puppy, encased in its membranous bag, will be passed. Most bitches will bite through this bag (it is sometimes ruptured at birth), so allowing the puppy to breathe. Very young bitches, however, will sometimes treat the encapsulated puppy with bewilderment, and with the oxygen supply from the bitch having ceased, the puppy will soon die in his watery capsule. Sometimes this bag therefore needs to be ripped open, and the convulsions of the puppy will usually awaken maternal instincts in the bitch, causing her to lick the puppy clean and dry, thereby also stimulating the puppy's body functions.

Parturition problems are rare in lurchers and greyhounds. Not only are the breeds literally free from the abnormalities of some of the show breeds, as I have already said, but also the heads of lurcher puppies are usually quite small, and therefore little difficulty is experienced in passing such puppies. On the other hand, the hundred to one chance can come up and the bitch may have trouble whelping. The reasons for this happening can be many. First, the bitch may have a pelvic deformity which prevents normal parturition, though this is extremely rare in greyhound types of dog. Secondly, a very large puppy may be jamming the birth canal, thus making birth difficult. Thirdly and lastly, the bitch may be utterly exhausted by the time the last few puppies are to be born, for greyhound types of dog tend to have large litters, and the condition known as uterine inertia – literally, a tiring of the womb – may prevent further births. The time between puppies should be watched and noted, and should a lapse of two or three hours take place between the whelping of each puppy, the breeder will know there is some cause for concern. Like as not the cause is uterine inertia, and this can only be remedied by an injection of Pituitrin, given by a vet. It is certainly not a job for an amateur, however gifted he may be with dogs. The use of Pituitrin during parturition has, in fact, been described as like adjusting one's carburettor with a sledgehammer. Within half an hour of the injection, the bitch will experience violent contractions of the uterus – violent enough to push even a big puppy out into the world. Should this injection fail, however, then the breeder must face the prospect of a Caesarean section to release the puppies.

Talk of a Caesarean section usually fills most dog breeders with dread, but, provided the bitch is not totally exhausted by fruitless contractions, the operation is relatively uncomplicated and the bitch will suffer little from the surgery. Obviously this is a job for a vet, but most vets find little trouble in surgery of this nature. An incision is made in the uterus wall, and the puppies are taken out with veterinary forceps, after which the surgeon will sew up the uterus wall and then the walls of the abdomen. It is a relatively simple and usually most successful operation, but it should be used only as a last resort once natural methods and the use of Pituitrin have failed to take effect. Again, it must be stressed that such operations are rarely needed in breeding lurchers, and the bitch will most probably whelp during the night with a minimum of fuss and problems.

The question of artificial heat during whelping is always something of a talking point, though the answer is obvious. A bitch whelped in a warm house will usually require little heat, but a bitch whelped in a shed, particularly during winter time, will almost certainly need some form of artificial heat if she is to rear her puppies properly. Many claim that survival of the fittest should be practised, and the bitch allowed to rear only the puppies that survive the chill of the first hours of birth. It is for this very reason that it is madness to imagine that buying puppies from tinkers and gipsies can ever be a good bet. Puppies born in spartan conditions under caravans rarely do well and never overcome the disadvantages of their birth.

In winter time, heat is essential or losses will be high. The temperature in the uterus of a bitch is 101.5°F (38.5°C), and to bring the puppies into a world of practically zero temperature is to ask for trouble. People who advocate harsh conditions are frankly usually too mean to provide heat for the dog, and are certainly not motivated by stoical philosophies or reason. Furthermore, it is worth mentioning that no puppy benefits from being chilled and many carry the ill-effects of such shock treatment for life. Because a lurcher is bred to be a canine athlete, the long-distance runner of the dog world, he needs all the help he can get to grow into a healthy, active dog. Puppies reared in cold conditions are not worth the purchasing, and puppies with bulging eyes, pot bellies and fleshless ribs all provide a fair illustration of their breeder's ignorance or meanness. It is also a public health regulation that the dog breeder – by definition, one who owns more than two breeding bitches – must provide heat for puppy rearing. Losses among winter-whelped puppies are appalling if no heat is provided, and the purchase of a heat lamp, cables and the cost of electricity will be more than compensated by the rearing of just one extra puppy.

I am somewhat against culling a litter, as Walsh suggests one should do in *Lurchers and Long Dogs*. He states that a large litter should be culled to a manageable number, six seeming reasonable, and that the majority of males in the litter should be put down. This does, of course, give the remaining puppies a better chance of thriving, for not only will each get more milk, but they will also benefit from the extra individual attention the dam can give them. It must be remembered, however, that, at three weeks of age, a puppy is taking most of its food in the form of macerated or regurgitated meat from the bitch, so the bitch has only a short time to feed her litter through her body milk, though she will actually continue to suckle them until they are five or six weeks old. A strong, healthy bitch, well fed (but not over-fed) during pregnancy, will be more than able to cope with all her puppies, particularly if she is given extra food from the time the whelps are born. This is the correct and suitable time to cram the bitch with as much food as she can eat.

Normally, immediately after whelping, a bitch is glutted with the placenta and the wrapping of the puppy. She will usually pass black-green, tarry faeces the next day as a result of this ingestion, but on no account should she be prevented from eating what may seem to us to be the rather unpleasant mess of cauls and afterbirth. Not only is it a natural way to get rid of the trappings of birth, but the ingestion of such stuff is believed to stimulate the development of milk in a bitch. It certainly stimulates the action of the bowels and cleans out various impurities from the alimentary tract. From this time on, however, she should have as much food as she wants, and the food must be of a suitable kind. Meat is the ideal diet for the nursing bitch (and for all dogs, for that matter), and the more meat she gets the better her puppies will grow. Any form of flesh is useful, though I avoid using lights and spleen because of their laxative qualities.

This is one time where I would advise feeding whole, small carcasses: rabbits, hares, turkeys, hens and so on. Yes, small bones as well, contrary to the advice of most books, whose writers throw up their hands in horror at the prospect of feeding dogs with tiny bones that can splinter. The carcasses of small mammals or birds are easily digested by a dog of lurcher type, and during the years that I have bred dogs I have never encountered anything but good results from whole-carcass feeding. Fur and feather binding, as a consequence of the indigestible material clogging the gut, is a very rare condition in healthy lurchers. In other dogs, corrupted and deformed by breeding for the show bench, such a diet may cause trouble, but not, most certainly, in a breed as vigorous as the lurcher. Few gipsy dogs are fed, and they mostly fend for themselves, eating rabbits, hares, rats and God knows what, yet few seem to suffer from their diet. Failing whole carcasses, beef, horse meat, paunch, tripe and butcher's waste will generally suffice. Chicken entrails, though frequently worm-riddled, will also make nourishing food.

Towards the end of the second week of the rearing of the puppies, it will be observed that the bitch, particularly if she is a collie hybrid, will literally fill her belly at the dinner plate, and then regurgitate the meat right on top of her puppies. This habit, though seemingly quite nauseating (for half-digested meat stinks with the sort of sweetness one associates with decay), should not be discouraged. It is a relic of the time when wild dogs brought back the meat in the most convenient receptacles to hand: namely, their own stomachs. This half-digested meat, though unpleasant to humans, is most enticing food for puppies not yet weaned, for not only is it easy to suck, but is fairly well macerated by this time and in such a state of partial digestion that some of the nutrients are soluble and thus easily assimilated.

As soon as one observes puppies sucking at this nauseous mess, one should consider getting them weaned. The best first solid food is flesh, but flesh devoid of the sinews and cellular tissue of meat straight from the butcher's slab. Scraped meat – meat scraped with a knife until it yields a bloody pulp – is totally digestible and fairly irresistible to any puppy, and hence is ideal. It should be offered by rubbing a tiny portion against the lips and gums, and if the puppy is ready to wean, it will usually suck at the pulp almost frantically. Similarly, a pulverized kidney will send a puppy berserk with excitement. Should the puppy display no interest in the food offered, the breeder should not force it to take flesh, but simply try it with flesh again the next day. If it refuses it again, offer it once more the next day and the next day, until the time comes when it eats it enthusiastically. Once the puppies have started to eat, they should be fed copious amounts of flesh as well as milk food. Get into the habit of feeding puppies at the same times each day, little and often being better than large meals once a day.

By the time the puppies are three weeks old, the breeder should contemplate worming the litter. Advice: avoid like the plague old wives' remedies advocated by pseudo-authorities – remedies often guaranteed to send a puppy to the grave, its belly still distended with roundworms. Gipsy and tinker nostrums can be deadly. Our local band of itinerants once advised me to worm my puppies with a mixture of ground glass and syrup! Another group came forth with the hoary oldie of putting a wad of chewing tobacco down the throats of the puppies. On reflection, perhaps these remedies were suggested to prevent me rearing the litter. Pattinson speaks highly of gipsy-reared dogs in Devon, and maybe the gipsy of the Midlands is different in style from the Devonshire variety, but I have certainly seen animals kept in disgusting conditions on tinker sites, and from my own experience would say that the only difference between tinkers and gipsies so far as dogs are concerned is that the latter will give you bad advice in Romany.

Vets are the people to advise about parasites and their eradication (and I deal specifically with tapeworms on pages 181-2). Before the discovery of the drug piperazine citrate, old-fashioned roundworm remedies could be very dangerous and unreliable. Santonin, a chemical used in the period immediately after the Second World War, really could injure a weak and off-colour puppy, though it certainly got rid of worms. Modern remedies for roundworms use piperazine citrate as the active ingredient, and there are little or no side-effects when this chemical is used. Shaw's Erliworm is an excellent buffered solution of this chemical, and it can be given to puppies as young as three weeks. Worming is not only good for the litter, it is essential. Not only do worms eat up a great deal of the dog's food, but they are also injurious in other ways. Worms prevent themselves from being digested by secreting a toxic slime, and when this is absorbed by the dog it can cause serious illnesses. The roundworm is also capable of infecting humans, particularly small children, and causing an unpleasant and sometimes fatal illness called viceral larval migrans. Until the puppies have been wormed, it is inadvisable for a breeder to allow children to touch them.

A puppy dosed with piperazine citrate will pass a stool that is literally 80 per cent worms, all of which will be dead or in the process of dying at the time of passing. Burn all stools and forgo any morbid desire to uncoil the lengths of tissue. The eggs in the faeces, unharmed by the piperazine, will adhere to your skin and become ingested or find entry to the body in some other way. Two or three wormings at three-weekly intervals will certainly get rid of most worms.

One point before leaving the subject of worming. If he worms puppies at three weeks old, then the breeder will find no worms in the puppies' faeces, for he will not, in fact, find the puppies' faeces at all. Bitches are usually fairly meticulous about cleaning up their puppies, and consequently eat the faeces of puppies until the puppy is about six weeks old. Examination of the bitch's stools will usually reveal massive worms curled like springs. It is wise to note that no dog is ever completely free from worms, for ascarids, or roundworms, live out their life cycle in various parts of the dog's anatomy. Some breeders worm a bitch for roundworms when she is three or four weeks pregnant, in the belief that this will reduce the number of worms eventually found in the puppies. While it does not harm, I am not wholly convinced that it helps to eradicate worms in either bitch or puppies.

Provided the bitch is healthy and well fed during pregnancy and nursing, she will experience no problems in rearing her puppies. Sometimes, however, things do go amiss. One of the most serious and dangerous maladies that can beset a nursing bitch is hypercalcaemia, called eclampsia in most dog books, though in fact it is nothing of the sort. Hypercalcaemia, or milk fever, is quite common in smaller breeds, but it can occur in greyhounds and lurchers. It is a consequence of calcium salts being lost to the bitch's body by the puppies' suckling, for dog milk is especially rich in calcium. The first signs that this malady is about to strike is the sight of the bitch moving with a jerky walk, her feet literally clattering on hard ground. Later she will begin to sway drunkenly, and if the ailment is allowed to proceed, she will pass into one of the most dramatic fits the owner is likely to see, thrashing around her pen, paddling her legs like a thing possessed. The treatment and cure is almost as dramatic, though the amateur breeder should consult a vet as soon as possible, and, in fact, the moment he notices the first symptoms. Unless he is reasonably quick about getting professional aid, his failure to do so will result in the death of the bitch. Most unaccountable deaths during nursing are the result of milk fever.

Treatment consists of intravenal injections of a chemical called calcium boroglutinate. Within seconds of the needle entering the vein, the bitch will appear to come round, sometimes biting at the hypodermic needle. Hypercalcaemia, or the tendency to it, appears to be hereditary, and is associated with big litters which quickly drain all the calcium from the bitch. It is futile to feed calcium in the form of bone meal or calcium lactate during either pregnancy or nursing. Such calcium will not be absorbed by the bitch, but will merely dissolve in the stomach, being reprecipitated in the gut and causing fearful constipation. All one can do is watch for the onset of the malady from the ninth day after whelping until the time when the puppies are weaned. Immediate treatment is necessary and there are no short cuts.

Fortunately, it is a disease that is uncommon in large breeds.

Puppies should be ready to leave the bitch at seven or eight weeks of age, though personally I wean my puppies far sooner as I am keen to begin their training and socializing. Eight weeks is, however, a suitable age to wean and sell a litter. Do not be pressurized by your high feed bill into selling puppies any earlier, though I confess that a lurcher litter can eat one out of house and home. Puppies sold at four or five weeks may do well in the hands of people who have expertise in dog rearing, but the amateur or untrained dog keeper (and frankly, most lurcher owners come into this category), will usually have trouble rearing such a young puppy. Invariably the puppy will be beset by stomach disorders and chronic diarrhoea which will set him behind any brothers and sisters who have stayed with their dam.

Sell to whomever you wish, but try to ensure that the puppy will get a good and, above all, permanent home. So many lurcher keepers are flash-in-the-pan stockmen who have lurchers at one moment and bantams and pigeons the next, lurchers therefore tending to change hands at the devil of a rate. In the Midlands, the average lurcherman will usually be quite proud to say that he has owned a particular lurcher dog for a year or two. Frequent changes in the dog's life don't help its psychological development, and most dogs which change hands regularly finish up in fairly terrible conditions within a few years. I dread having lurchers stolen, for I know they will usually die under some caravan or other in somewhat appalling conditions. Try to ensure that your puppy goes to a reasonably good home and to reasonably enlightened people. If you breed good stock and rear it well, the chances are you will be able to choose your purchaser and reject anyone who seems unsuitable.

Regarding the price one should charge for a puppy, this is a question on which there appears to be no hard and fast rule. Prices range from £5 to £50, but it is as well to remember that a person usually gets what he pays for. I should be careful about purchasing a puppy for £5, which is far less than the price of rearing it. Likewise, I should like to see both parents (and observe their performance) where a puppy is for sale at £50. Too low a price will attract an amazing variety of riff-raff, ranging from dealers to sheer lunatics, lunatics being all too common in the lurcher fraternity. Similarly, £50 will attract the curious and the time-waster who will take up your entire day asking all sorts of damn-fool questions and finally leave telling you that they will let you know.

Time-wasters abound in lurcher circles, for many lurchermen are, sad to say, shiftless non-workers who have all the time in the world at their disposal. Furthermore, an advertisement for a puppy will always, and I mean *always*, attract an undesirable type of person interested in buying a grown, trained dog, or a dog already doing a bit – the type of person who sets my teeth on edge and puts me in a bad humour for days afterwards. The standard of lurcher training required by most people is very low, so anyone who wants to buy a trained, or started, dog is either themselves a complete failure at dog training or a half-wit. To sell a dog to either type would be foolish and irresponsible, and it usually results in the buyer returning your dog damaged with a cryptic comment, 'N'good.' Furthermore, what on earth are you doing selling a grown dog, or a partly entered dog? Only a fool would part with such an animal.

As the breeder gains more experience of both dogs and men, he will be able to spot on sight the obvious time-waster or the lunatic who asks for a puppy on trial, the person who has just a few pounds short of the price you are asking or the bidder who will try and beat down your price (he will also be pretty mean about feeding his dogs, you can be sure). Genuine buyers will make their purchase, pay their money and depart. The character who hangs around, shows you photographs of his saluki, collie or whatnot and generally makes a pest of himself, can waste an entire day. Furthermore, do not hesitate to deter unlikely or undesirable purchasers. I am, I confess, very anti-itinerant, for unlike Pattinson I live near a travellers' site and see some appalling things, enough to convince anyone that the RSPCA would do well to earn their money by frequenting such places. Place your price too high, say the puppies are already sold, do anything so long as you don't sell to someone who is obviously unsuitable.

Before leaving the subject of lurcher breeding, it is perhaps wise to debunk the old wives' tale of telegony. Example: a greyhound bitch gets out and is mated by a cur. The litter is born and the puppies are clearly mongrels. Subsequently, the greyhound bitch rears her litter, comes into season again and is mated by a greyhound. It is a piece of superstitious nonsense that this and subsequent litters will be ruined by the fact that the bitch has been served by a mongrel earlier in her life, but many still believe it to be a fact. The puppies from the first mating will be mongrels or lurchers, call them what you will, but the bitch's subsequent litters will in no way be influenced by her first misalliance. The origin of the theory of telegony is curious and highly unscientific but space does not permit a treatise on such foolishness.

12 *Diseases and Precautions*

To begin with, the lurcher, derived as it is from the greyhound, is practically free from genetic deformities and weaknesses. Greyhounds, and to a certain extent lurchers, have been bred from the toughest, fastest and the most physically perfect specimens. The good have been used for breeding, and the inferior – well, they have gone to the wall. Such a survival-of-the-fittest programme has produced the paragon of athletic ability that we call the greyhound, one of the few large dogs not plagued with the curse of patella luxation, hip dysplacia or other ailments all too common in the dog world. Free from genetic faults lurchers and running dogs may be, but free from disease they certainly are not, and any lurcher breeder or trainer worth his salt should be able to recognize such problems and, if he cannot bring about a cure, at least know enough to get a vet and have his dog treated. At the time of writing, few lurchermen have such knowledge, and the sight of mangy, worm-infested dogs is all too common at lurcher shows. If this book does nothing else, I hope it will alleviate the distress of some of our most useful animals.

For the sake of convenience, let us divide the subject of disease into two categories: (a) diseases which can be fatal, and (b) diseases which cause discomfort and distress. (For postnatal hypercalcaemia, see pages 167-8.)

Lethal Infections

Distemper and Hard Pad

With the exception of rabies, which, thank God, has not to date arrived in our country, the most deadly canine infection is undoubtedly distemper. Distemper is a relatively new disease for British dogs, for it first reared its ugly head in the eighteenth century and was undoubtedly introduced by French aristocrats escaping the guillotine. To judge by the effects of the disease which I have observed, it might perhaps have been preferable for the self-same aristocrats to have stayed to face the blade, for distemper is the very devil of an infection and often absolutely lethal to a dog. Distemper, along with hard pad, which is only a slightly different variety of distemper, is not a disease as such, but quite simply a whole mess of diseases caused by viruses that closely resemble one another. The symptoms of these diseases – hard pad included – are so similar that they may be considered and treated as the same disease. In 1958, Laidlaw and Dunkin divided the distemper viruses into three main types. Virus A is a particularly lethal brand of the disease, which, incidentally, once hit my own kennels. Virus B is an uncommon variety, whose effects are rather less fatal than Virus A. And Virus C is a type of distemper scarcely injurious, and hardly more harmful than the common cold. Dogs usually recover from the C virus with little damage to their systems, other than, perhaps, a slight tarnishing and pitting of the teeth.

The disease commences its cycle insidiously. The dog may one day appear to be off-colour and display a reluctance to exercise or play. A dog who has an excellent hunting record will suddenly make a surprisingly half-hearted attempt at taking quarry. Within hours of this lassitude, the eyes of the infected dog will be gummed up and the nose will usually be dry and fairly warm (this is how the theory of a cold, damp nose being symptomatic of health in a dog originated, for, when the disease first hit Britain, the death rate was alarming enough to make dog owners especially aware of the symptoms of distemper). The dog's temperature may soar well above the normal 101.5°F (38.5°C), and the dog will be unwilling to take food or drink. Diarrhoea will often accompany the disease, and this, coupled with the dog's reluctance to drink, will produce a pitifully emaciated wreck within a few days: a dog resembling a dehydrated bag of bones is often the result of a distemper attack. Sometimes spots or a rash will be seen on the belly – but take care with this symptom, for most lurchers who work hard through nettles or cover will display a rash brought on by irritation set up by brambles and suchlike.

What is even more unpleasant about this disease is that the dog may appear to recover from the infection and seem to become hale and hearty again, only to relapse into a threshing fit a few days later. When fits like these accompany the course of the disease, brain damage, paralysis and nervous diseases such as chorea (a twitching of the legs – an uncontrollable shaking action comparable to St Vitus's dance in humans) are often the results of the infection. Such disorders render the lurcher, or any other type of dog, useless, and it is frankly kinder to destroy such an animal as painlessly as possible than to allow it to continue in this state. Any running dog with these symptoms would certainly feel like a bird with its wings clipped.

The cure for such an infection? There simply isn't one. The dog breeder who could back his claim to have one – and the sporting books are packed with lunatic advice – would be a clever man indeed. Research laboratories like Burroughs Wellcome have failed to come up with anything significant, so it is unlikely that the average lurcherman can advise you about treatment. The only honest advice possible is to keep the patient warm and offer up a prayer to any patron saint of dogs. Futile perhaps, but no more ludicrous than the advice often proffered by supposed experts. Sundry lunatic remedies abound. One theory is that a collar painted in Stockholm tar will keep the disease at bay, but the same was said of the Black Death, and collars proved equally ineffective at keeping that disease under control. In any case, while plague fleas might just possibly be deterred by this pungent substance, viruses have no sense of smell. Lucas, in his otherwise estimable book, *Hunt and Working Terriers*, mentions how he played a part in creating a medicine called Lucanis, supposedly highly effective in the control of distemper. Sadly, he was quite mistaken about this nostrum – it has little or no effect on the progress of the disease. Neither do any antibiotics help the infection, though they may well help to clear up secondary bacterial infections which the dog picks up in his low condition.

So the picture is gloomy indeed so long as a dog is uninoculated. Few unprotected dogs recover totally from this infection to become as fit and well as they were before its commencement. Inoculation is therefore essential. Normally this consists of injecting the dog with a weakened virus when the animal is twelve weeks old. A puppy under that age is still influenced by the antibodies it has acquired from suckling the colostrum, or first milk, from its mother, and these antibodies usually interfere with the processes the dog uses to cope with the virus. In times of danger, however, a puppy can often be inoculated considerably earlier. During an infection that hit my kennels in 1974, I lost nearly every puppy before it was six weeks of age, though my inoculated adult stock remained untroubled by the disease. Eventually I inoculated all puppies at seventeen days old, and thus the disease was finally stamped out, but, in the process of learning this control method, I lost nearly a hundred terrier and lurcher puppies.

Under normal circumstances, as I say, vets will delay inoculation for distemper until a puppy is twelve weeks of age. This method leaves a puppy vulnerable to infection until the bitch's antibodies (passed via the colostrum) are used up. Vets therefore use a measles vaccine if there should be any danger from a puppy having been in contact with a distemperous dog. The measles virus closely resembles the distemper bug, and prevents infection by a principle known as blocking. That is, the measles virus fills the cells, thereby preventing the distemper bug from invading the tissue. As a distemper preventative, the measles vaccine has proved most reliable, though I must admit I had little success when I used it to combat my distemper outbreak in 1974. Any infection that could just possibly be distemper needs veterinary attention, and the dog keeper would do well to avoid all well-wishers with quack medicines. Prevention is far better than cure, and inoculation is the only way to guard a dog against being infected.

Before leaving the subject of distemper, it is of interest to note that ferrets also die from distemper, and do so far more quickly than any dog. The mustelid family all seem totally unable to develop any immunity to the infection, and a distemper outbreak in kennels, even a mild Virus C outbreak, will usually mean the loss of the entire ferretry. Ferrets in fact act as a sort of early warning device in a kennels, rather as the miner's canary acts in the pit, for the first hint of distemper will usually see the deaths of a number of them. Ferrets, too, can and should be inoculated against distemper. A vet will usually use one dose of canine distemper vaccine to inoculate five ferrets, so the protection of both dogs and ferrets is relatively inexpensive.

Hard pad, incidentally, is merely a type of distemper, a particularly virulent form admittedly, but distemper nevertheless. All distemper vaccinations will protect a dog from hard pad. The bug gets its name from the fact that it causes the soles of the feet to thicken and harden (and also causes the nostrils to become like leather). Hard pad also infects ferrets.

Infectious Hepatitis or Rhubarth's Disease

This is a disease of the liver, and it is also deadly. Before describing the disease and its treatment, it is as well to remind the reader that the liver controls many bodily functions, such as the breakdown of damaged or ageing blood corpuscles, the destruction of toxic waste in the body and the processing of protein types of material. Hence a malfunction of this organ can, and does, have massive repercussions. Again the disease is caused by a virus, so antibiotics have little or no effect on its progress.

The sources of infection are many. It is communicable from dog to dog, simply by each animal sniffing the anus or genitals of the others, as all dogs are prone to do, or by sniffing lamp-posts or other marking points that have been soiled by the urine of other dogs. Whatever the method of communication, the effect is the same, for hepatitis can not only kill, but kill very quickly. Old poachers who never inoculated their dogs will usually tell stories of old So-and-so's Nip or Jade who died mysteriously in his sleep after an illness lasting only a matter of hours. This illness was probably hepatitis.

174

The symptoms are somewhat vague and variable. The dog may stroll around, a picture of apathy and dejection, and even bump into objects. Fits and the most hellish convulsions are not uncommon, all sorts of toxic waste being absorbed by the body as soon as the liver is failing to function correctly. High temperatures frequently occur, and the loss of weight is frighteningly rapid, the dog becoming an emaciated wreck in a matter of hours. Dogs will often act strangely and become comatose. Sometimes a dog vomits and has very bad diarrhoea. Invariably, however, jaundice manifests itself, a symptom of any disease of the liver, for the icterus, or yellowing, merely indicates a disturbance of the liver. The symptoms are, in fact, closely similar to those of leptospiral jaundice (see below).

Losses are high, particularly in puppies, and adult dogs will almost certainly die once they are infected. Old keepers used to say that a dog would probably survive if it was still alive a week after the infection, and there is more than a grain of truth in the statement, for the disease progresses rapidly and few dogs survive an infection longer than six days. The danger is, of course, that a dog who does get better will excrete the live virus in its urine for many months after recovering from the disease.

The treatment is fairly unsatisfactory, and usually consists of injections of antibiotics, which are of little use against the virus but a help against secondary infections. Anti-serum and injections of glucose and vitamin K will also be given. Veterinary research has shown, however, that a dog who is infected stands very little chance of survival, particularly if the owner is not familiar with the early symptoms of the disease.

Inoculation of puppies at twelve weeks old is essential and provides an almost certain preventative against hepatitis. It is also a damn-sight cheaper than the cost of months of veterinary treatment that will follow an outbreak of the disease.

Leptospiral Jaundice

This is yet another lethal infection, and it is far more common than most people realize. Recently research teams have shown that the disease is passed on by most rodents, and these include moles, mice and hamsters, though, of course, the arch-harbourer of leptospiral jaundice is that ubiquitous little disease merchant, the brown rat. The research findings have shown that 55 per cent of all rats carry this hellish infection, or, to put it another way, if your dog bites a rat he has a fifty-fifty chance of contracting the disease. Actually he does not even have to bite a rat, for all that is necessary is for him to eat food soiled by rat urine or merely to ingest material from where a rat has run. Before the reader slams the book shut at this point, stating indignantly that his dog never goes near a rat, may I mention that there are few corners of Britain where rats are not present, either as inhabitants or migrants. Open fields are frequently thoroughfares for rats in transit, and the germ that causes the infection can live for some time on grass or dry soil.

Having outlined how the disease is caused, let us now examine the symptoms, and again they are quite similar to hepatitis. The dog looks sick and decidedly lethargic. Half-way through a course, or even during a walk, he will simply give up and appear exhausted. His belly will seem to be tucked up, his eyes will look dull and unintelligent. Vomiting will usually follow the early symptoms, and dehydration of the body will be clearly evident in a matter of hours. (There is an easy test for dehydration, incidentally. The skin of the normal, healthy dog will, if grabbed behind the neck, resume its normal shape almost immediately it is released. In a dehydrated dog, the flesh will slide back very slowly.) Next the disease will attack the liver, causing the bile duct to fail to discharge its pigment into the gut. Subsequently the faeces become white or putty coloured. Then, as the pigment is reabsorbed by the bloodstream, the eyes, gums and belly of the dog grow canary yellow. Next the faeces become tarry and black, not because the liver has resumed its normal function, but because faeces of this type indicate a bleeding in the gut. Such a haemorrhage stains the stools and imparts a fearsome stench to the droppings. It is possible to detect the kennels of a badly infected dog some forty to fifty feet away, and it is the most indescribable stink; the smell of death and corruption comes near to describing it, however, and death and corruption will invariably follow if the disease is left to run its course. Death usually follows within ten days of the onset of the infection.

Again, treatment is not only expensive, but usually unsuccessful. Avoid like the plague the advice of well-wishers who lack veterinary knowledge, and seek professional help the moment the dog is off-colour. Anti-serum will sometimes help, as will large doses of antibiotic. Saline injections, and really massive injections too, are usually necessary to prevent dehydration. Even if the dog recovers, he is capable of transmitting the disease by way of his urine for many months, and transmitting it not only to other dogs, but also to humans, for leptospiral jaundice is synonymous with Weil's disease, one of the most unpleasant and deadly infections known to man.

A far more simple control is to inoculate the dog at twelve weeks old, booster injections then being necessary once a year if the dog is to remain completely immunized against this deadly disease.

Canicola Fever

This disease resembles leptospiral jaundice closely, and is also a lot more common than most people believe. One survey conducted on dogs allowed to roam the streets in Glasgow revealed that 40 per cent of all the street dogs had been infected at some time in their lives with canicola fever and had tissues damaged by the disease. It is another disease that can infect human beings as well as dogs.

Symptoms may vary from dog to dog. Some display acute jaundice, others develop fetid breath and vomiting. It is a disease that can cripple dogs through kidney damage, and many dogs die from canicola fever within a year or two of appearing to have recovered from the infection. It is far easier to prevent the disease than to cure it. Inoculation is again the answer.

Minor Common Ailments

Mange

Basically there are two distinct types of mange: *sarcoptic mange* and *follicular mange*. Both cause hair loss, and only an expert can distinguish between the two.

Sarcoptic mange: This disease is caused by a tiny crab-shaped mite called *Sarcoptes scabii*, or a similar mite called *Sarcoptes communis*, though the latter is more frequently found on rats and foxes than on dogs. Mange in its sarcoptic variety is symptomatic of poor kennel craft and neglect, yet many dogs at lurcher shows are infected with this mite. The same mite causes human scabies, so it is highly foolish not to treat a dog immediately sarcoptic mange is suspected.

The symptoms of the infection are fairly obvious. The dog is perpetually scratching, usually, at first, at areas around the eyes and ears. Hair loss is evident within a few days of the outbreak, and the skin beneath the hair grows inflamed. Other areas now become infected, and raw inflamed patches appear on the body and legs. If it is left to run its course, and it goes without saying that it never should be, mange will render a dog hairless and the skin a suppurating mess, for staphylococcus bugs will invade every scratch wound. I have seen two extreme cases of mange, both on lurchers, and both of whose owners were worthy of prosecution for cruelty. Sadly, mange is commonly present in lurcher kennels, partly because of the bad conditions in which many lurchermen keep their animals, and partly because of the immense

177

amount of dealing there is in the lurcher fraternity which helps to speed up the spread of the disease.

The treatment is lengthy, and very lengthy indeed if one aims totally to eradicate the mange mite. The first priority is hygiene. The shed should be scrubbed thoroughly with a strong solution of washing soda to start with, and this dissolves all the grease on the walls and floors. Then it should be scrubbed with bleach solution, the chlorine in which destroy all pests living in the shed. Allow the shed to dry and air before replacing the dogs. Concrete sheds and similar structures should be fumigated with a BHC fumigation capsule, or, better still, by burning a paste made of three parts sulphur and one part methylated spirits. Allow a full day before reintroducing the dog. This treatment will ensure the destruction of mange parasites living in crevices – mange parasites which would soon reinfect the dog. Weekly shed hygiene should be practised if one is totally to eradicate mange.

As for the treatment of the dog itself, old remedies suggest a mixture of sulphur and grease – messy, but reasonably effective. Dips in a solution of liver of sulphur help to clear up the infection, though few people relish using this liquid because of its pungent, rotten-eggs smell. Proprietary mange dips, which usually contain gamma benzene hexachloride (gamma BHC) are also effective, though during the past few years mange strains that are resistant to BHC have appeared. Benzyl benzoate was once in favour as a treatment, but latterly is not so fashionable, partly, I suppose, because of the erythema, or skin reddening, caused on human patients who are being treated for scabies. Regardless of the problems caused by this chemical, and they are usually quite minor problems, benzyl benzoate is still perhaps the best mangicide. Care should be taken not to cover the dog completely in the emulsion or death can result. Treating half the dog on one day and the other half on the next day is the treatment usually advised.

During the past ten years, sulphur-based chemicals have been found to be very effective. Selenium sulphide is one that has had good results in combating mange. Tetmosol, another sulphur-based compound, is also used, but the dog owner should follow the maker's advice to the letter when using this chemical for it is extremely toxic. Continue mange treatment until well after the infection has passed, and weekly dips in mangicide will prevent its reappearance. Kennel hygiene must, however, be kept to a very high level if the problem is not to present itself again.

Follicular mange: This is a more baffling disease, and while many nostrums and medicines appear on the market from time to time, few, if any, help to eradicate it. It is caused by a degenerate cigar-shaped mite that burrows beneath the skin and lives in the fatty subcutaneous tissue of the dog. Hence it is difficult to kill, and hence the disease is very difficult to cure. Some strains of dog are particularly prone to follicular mange infection, and several strains of dachshund have become very nearly extinct as a result of it, though whether the tendency to the disease is inherited or whether the actual mite is contracted by the puppies when suckling is still debatable. Sufficient to say that greyhounds are also prone to the infection, as are smooth-coated lurchers, though rough-coated lurchers are for some reason or other rarely troubled by this mite.

The symptoms of the disease are many. First there will be little or no scratching, but the hair follicles will simply fall out and the skin become grey and leathery, resembling the skin of an elephant calf. Sometimes the skin becomes flaky, and sometimes pustular eruptions are noticed.

As to treatment, most methods, as I say, are totally ineffective since the mite lies protected just beneath the skin of the dog. Systemic insecticides – insecticides taken either orally or injected subcutane-ously – are often tried, but even these seem to have little effect on the mite. Medicated baths have a slight effect, some of the sulphides being absorbed through the skin, but again the effect is fairly negligible. Perhaps the only advice that can be given sounds rather negative, but it is useful just the same. Follicular mange seems to infect dogs that are a bit off-colour, a bit below par, either through a lowered condition or simply by extra stress, as in pregnancy or teething. Dogs who develop the infection should be kept in high condition and be given tonics containing tiny amounts of arsenic as soon as the condition appears to form. As a matter of interest, dogs infected with this type of mange can be kennelled with other dogs without danger of infecting the healthy animals, whereas sarcoptic mange will spread like wildfire through a kennels.

Eczema

Mange and eczema look very alike to the layman, and even a veterinary surgeon needs to take skin scrapings to determine which is which. Eczema is caused by allergies, or is sometimes simply the result of a nervous complaint. Many dogs develop eczema when fed fish. Others are allergic to cereal meals. Eczema perhaps indicates that a change of diet is necessary, but it can also sometimes be rectified by allowing the dog access to green foods, and it sometimes clears if the dog is given the freedom of a grass run. Should the disease persist, consult a veterinary surgeon, but, be warned, the treatment is long and often expensive.

Wounds

Imagine a dog racing at speeds approaching 30 miles an hour, often in the dark, through the typical English countryside, scattered, as it is, with thorns, stumps, gates with nails and, horror of horrors, barbed wire. Sooner or later that dog is going to be quite badly torn, and its owner will certainly need some knowledge of how to treat the wounds. Even if a lurcher owner is totally oblivious to the ravages of mange and distemper, he must, of necessity, need to know a little about first aid.

Wounds fall into two categories. First come the rips and tears, such as are made by a dog dashing through a barbed-wire fence; and secondly there are punctures, such as are caused by nail wounds, slight contact with barbed wire or fox bites. Although these wounds may seem slight when compared with the rips and tears, they are far more open to infection. A rip will rarely fester, but a puncture invariably will if it is not treated.

Belly wounds, or rips near to the points of articulation – that is, at the joints of the hip and so on – need professional treatment and should never be tampered with. Stitching also needs to be done by a skilled person. Many amateur trainers profess to do their own stitching, and they possess dogs so criss-crossed with rips and tears as to look like sawmill accidents. A properly stitched wound usually leaves only a hairline scar, but a badly stitched rip looks frightful and amateurish. Furthermore, stitching needs to be done with a curved needle, not by the needle-and-thread job beloved of the ham-handed pseudo-experts.

First aid for wounds should consist of trimming the hair around the wound and cleaning with a proprietary disinfectant such as Dettol or TCP. Antibiotic tablets such as oxytetracycline are also advantageous as they promote inner healing. Abscesses can occur, particularly if the wound is overlooked, and such infections look far worse than they actually are. Many will swell to the size of cricket balls before bursting. Allow them to burst, however, and keep the wound open by bathing it with salt water while dosing the dog with oxytetracycline. As a matter of interest, old-fashioned remedies for abscesses recommend that the wound be kept open and flies allowed to lay their eggs in it. The resulting maggots gorge themselves on pus and necrotic flesh, thus cleaning out the wound. It is a very extreme measure, but I have seen it used and the wound certainly did heal up. It is obviously not a method that one would recommend, for it leaves scar tissue which is most unsightly as well as being quite unnecessary.

Ear Canker

This is quite simply any parasitic infection of the ears, and it is usually caused by a tiny mite called the otodectic mite. Its ravages nearly drive a dog mad and leave the ears open to any bacterial invasion which is going around. An infected dog shakes its head frantically, and a foul-smelling brown wax is usually found in the outer ear. Clean the ears with warm water and dose with a proprietary canker remedy, the best of which contain gamma BHC. If early treatment is neglected, expensive surgery will be needed to rectify the infection's ravages. Never pick or poke around in the animal's ears, but clean out the ears and treat them as advised. If this fails to clear the infection, consult a veterinary surgeon without further delay.

Worms

Roundworms: Roundworms have already been dealt with under the section concerned with breeding (pages 166-7 above).

Tapeworms: These are very common in lurchers, particularly in those animals which are allowed to wander the countryside, as are the dogs of itinerants. Such dogs ingest the faeces of sheep and with them the eggs of the tapeworm. Rabbit guts are also havens for tapeworms, and when fed uncooked to the dog can cause infection. Sheep paunches are also infested with these worms.

A dog infected with tapeworms will usually seem unwell and have a dull staring coat. Many drag their anus on the ground, though this may simply be a sign not of worms but of a blocked anal gland. Usually segments of the worms will be passed in the droppings, small pink or white pieces that wriggle convulsively for an hour or so after they are passed. This is the only way the layman can actually be sure that a dog is infected with worms. Some worms grow to gigantic size, ones 18 feet long having been recorded, though this is exceptional; and several worms are often hanging in the dog's bowels at the same time, attached to the gut wall by a hooked, head-like device known as the scolex. This worm produces toxic substances which harm a dog and they are best eradicated. Traditional gipsy folk medicine suggests that a few tapeworms are necessary to prevent a dog growing overweight. Disregard this advice and take steps to rid the dog of worms.

Worm medicine is easily obtainable. Most of the proprietary medicines today contain diphenalamine, which stuns the worms and allows the gut to digest them. No worms will be seen in the motions, simply a gelatinous substance. Personally I like the old remedies, such as Oil of Areca, which causes the worm to be expelled whole. Male fern capsules also cause the entire worm to be passed. These remedies are usually difficult to obtain and require that a dog should be fasted for a day before being given the worm remedies. Avoid like the plague the ground glass and chewing tobacco vermifuges which were often advised a century ago. While they certainly clear the worms, they also kill the dog.